Cost Management
for IT Services

IT Infrastructure Library

Brian Johnson

LONDON: THE STATIONERY OFFICE

CCTA

Central Computer and Telecommunications Agency

For further information regarding this
publication and other CCTA products
please contact:
Library
CCTA
Rosebery Court
St Andrews Business Park
Norwich NR7 0HS
Tel. 01603 704930

This document has been produced using
procedures conforming to
BSI 5750 Part 1: 1987; ISO 9001:1987

Table of contents

Foreword

Welcome to the IT Infrastructure Library module on
Cost Management for IT Services.

In their respective areas the IT Infrastructure Library
publications complement and provide more detail than the
IS Guides.

The ethos behind the development of the IT Infrastructure
Library is the recognition that organizations are becoming
increasingly dependent on IT in order to satisfy their
corporate aims and meet their business needs. This growing
dependency leads to growing requirement for quality IT
services. In this context quality means 'matched to business
needs and user requirements as these evolve'.

This module is one of a series of codes of practice intended
to facilitate the quality management of IT services and of
the IT Infrastructure. (By IT Infrastructure, we mean
organizations' computers and networks - hardware,
software and computer related communications, upon
which application systems and IT services are built and
run). The codes of practice will assist organizations to
provide quality IT services in the face of skill shortages,
system complexity, rapid change, growing user
expectations, current and future user requirements.

Underpinning the IT Infrastructure is the Environmental
Infrastructure upon which it is built. Environmental topics
are covered in separate sets of guides within the IT
Infrastructure Library.

IT infrastructure management is a complex subject which
for presentational and practical reasons has been broken
down within the IT Infrastructure Library into a series of
modules. A complete list of current and planned modules is
available from the CCTA IT Infrastructure Management
Services at the address given at the back of this module.

The structure of the module is, in essence:

* a **Management summary** aimed at senior managers
  (Directors of IT and above, typically down to Civil
  Service Grade 5), senior IT staff and, in some cases,
  users or office managers (typically Civil Service
  Grades 5 to 7)

* the main body of the text is aimed at IT middle
  management (typically grades 7 to HEO)

* technical detail in Annexes.

The module gives the main **guidance** in sections 3 to 5; explains the **benefits, costs and possible problems** in section 6, which may be of interest to senior staff; and provides information on **tools** (requirements and examples of real-life availability) in section 7.

CCTA is working with the IT industry to foster the development of software tools to underpin the guidance contained within the codes of practice (ie to make adherence to the module more practicable), and ultimately to automate functions.

If you have any comments on this or other modules, do please let us know. A **Comments sheet** is provided with every module. Alternatively you may wish to contact us directly using the reference point given in **Further information**.

Thank you. We hope you find this module useful.

Acknowledgement

The assistance of the following contributors is gratefully acknowledged.

Accountancy Advice Division, H M Treasury

Hans Dithmar (under contract to CCTA from CCMS).

1. Management summary

1.1 Background

IT services are commonly viewed as an important utility, but unfortunately and increasingly, as a free utility within the business organization. In addition, the ever increasing user base has caused IT Services budgets to grow and because of their complex nature, it is rare that the actual running costs of the IT services are properly identified.

The Cost Management for IT Services module addresses the main principles of management accounting required of the IT services directorate. The module discusses how IT Services management can design and implement a system for the accounting and apportionment of costs. Pricing policies and charging for IT services are also discussed.

The module specifically refers to infrastructure management costs, but the principles and advice applies to all aspects of IT Services (eg software development, in-house consultancy, procurement services and so on).

The module does not explicitly address placement of the costing and charging functions, ie whether the designing and running of the costing and charging functions should be predominantly in the hands of IT Services management, Finance Division or shared between them. For the purpose of the module, it is assumed that infrastructure management costing will be the responsibility of IT Services management. Placement will depend on what seems most appropriate for the organization concerned and will depend on decisions made regarding the scope of the project. If the organization intends to introduce cost management to charge for use of IT services, this is a strategic business decision. A similar decision will be required regarding placement of the function. Users are, inevitably, major contributors to strategic decisions and should be fully aware of the possible consequences of the installation and placement of an IT cost management system.

1.2 Purpose

The purpose of this module is to provide information about introducing a cost management system. The module states what needs to be done and discusses at a high level how it should be done, though examples provided in the annexes provide some detailed insight into practicalities.

Although this module of the IT Infrastructure Library refers to cost management in an IT environment, cost management is not special or peculiar to IT. Cost management applies throughout the organization and affects all management decisions whether personnel, transport or legal; even to the control of specific items such as stationery.

An effective cost management system should:

* provide assistance in developing a sound investment strategy which recognizes and evaluates the options and flexibility available from modern technology

* provide targets for performance and measure that performance against target. It should also enable management to monitor actual costs against budget

* facilitate prioritization of resource usage

* ensure the sound stewardship of all the assets employed in the organization, including the maintenance of appropriate records for control purposes and to support the stewardship

* assist management in their day-to-day decision making and enable them to make considered decisions as regards forward plans with the minimum of risk

* be flexible and capable of providing a fast response to changing business circumstances.

1.3   Aims

This module has three principal aims:

* to provide comprehensive guidance about the planning, implementation and operation of a costing and charging system from business evaluation through to running a fully operational cost management system

* to assist IT Services Managers to provide cost effective IT services, using the costing system to help ensure that the cost of providing the various services reflects real business needs, and using the charging system to provide income to the IT Services organization

* to promote the running of IT Services as a business operation.

1.4 Charging

The concept of accounting for costs is not new, but is becoming increasingly important. The concept of charging for incurred internal costs is, in Government at least, relatively new, but is one means of influencing use of resources. Introducing charges for IT services alone will, however, have little effect on resource use unless budget holders face similar charges for other services.

Full recovery of all expenditure is most often the reason for charging. In order to determine how much to charge for a service the real costs of providing the service must be known.

The essential objectives of charging are to:

* recover from users the full cost of (IT) services, including cost of capital

* ensure that (IT) users are aware of the costs which they impose on the (IT) systems

* ensure that (IT) providers have an incentive to deliver an agreed quality and quantity of economic and effective services.

Other objectives of charging are to:

* recover costs based on the amount of (IT) service usage

* shape customer behaviour (for example charging a different, lower, price for computer service at night is an incentive to use off-peak computer time for non-critical, or non-real-time work).

1.5 Benefits

The benefits of cost management for IT services are discussed in section 6. The principal benefits to be accrued from the introduction of IT costing include:

* accurate assessment of cost effectiveness criteria

* provision of information to justify IT investment

* the confidence with which plans can be made and budgets set.

The benefits of charging include:

* influencing customer behaviour toward the use of IT

* recovery of costs.

It is essential that the organization recognizes the inherent cost of introducing a cost management system, and that it is clear to the IT Services Directorate and business users what the introduction of the system is intended to achieve. Evaluation of costs and intentions is possible only if there is an understanding of the benefits (and problems) accrued through the introduction of a cost management system. Proper cost management will enable the organization to identify the real cost of providing and maintaining IT services for the business.

If charging for IT services is introduced, the charges can be based on accurate cost profiles so that the organization can be certain that its intentions about cost recovery (whether to break-even, to subsidize or to make profits at a predetermined target figure) can be achieved. Once again, however, it is essential that the organization is fully cognizant of the benefits and the pitfalls which follow on from the introduction of charging.

The cost information which will be available (together with information provided by capacity planners) will enable organizations to plan for investments and to control costs. Most importantly, the use of cost management lays the foundation for running IT Services as a business unit, which is not only customer-led but also accountable, cost conscious and forward looking.

2.   Introduction

2.1   Purpose

This module covers the management of, and charging for, IT services. The purpose is to provide guidance to IT Services Managers on how to implement and run a cost management system which allows:

* calculation of the cost of providing IT services

* identification and classification of the components of these costs

* apportionment and allocation of appropriate costs over the IT services provided to both internal and external customers

* implementation of equitable charging mechanisms for the use of IT services

* operation of the IT Services section as a business unit if required

* charges to be reviewed regularly to ensure they continue to reflect customer and business needs.

Such a system controls IT service costs and influences the proper use of IT resources, so that these scarce resources are used in the manner which best reflects business need.

2.2   Target readership

This module is aimed at IT directors, IT managers and their staff who are involved in managing the cost-effectiveness of IT service provision, and those responsible for cost-recovery and billing. In particular the target readership includes the IT Services Manager and the Cost Manager.

Ideally, an understanding of both IT and accountancy is required in order to implement the guidance: where accountancy expertise is not available, it is advisable to obtain consultancy from other directorates of the organization, or from external services.

2.3   Scope

The concepts of effective, economic and efficient provision of IT services are integral to Government policies of preparing IS strategies which accommodate the needs of the customers, the business and the organization. It could be argued that cost management, particularly in the instance of

Figure 1:
The role of
cost management

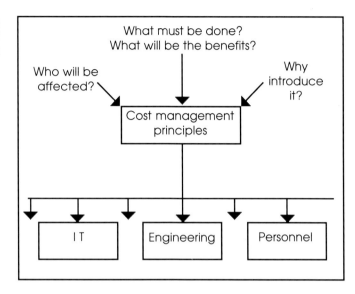

pricing policies, is one of the most important components of an IS strategy because pricing policies can shape the behaviour of customers towards their IT services.

Cost management issues permeate the entire organization and are not peculiar to IT. Figure 1 illustrates the role of cost management in an organization. The basic cost management principles (why do it, what to do and who it affects) are common. To a large extent, how to implement cost management is similar in different parts of the organization; but it is in the **how to** area that differences can be identified.

This module covers the general principles (why? what? who?) and provides guidance about how to design, implement and run an operational cost management system for IT services.

This module provides some background information about:

* the Financial Management Initiative (FMI) which represented the first major thrust to introduce modern corporate planning and financial management control arrangements into all areas of central Government

* the Next Steps initiative, which builds upon the development initiated in the FMI

* the budgeting process as the means of delegating control and monitoring performance against pre-defined targets

* pricing policies

* investment appraisal

* the control and audit of cost management systems.

2.3.1 Financial Management Initiative (FMI)

The Government's introduction of the FMI in 1982, brought greater responsibility and accountability of managers in the public sector to manage resources effectively, efficiently and economically within the parameters of predefined objectives and targets. An essential prerequisite to the successful achievement of managerial goals was seen to be greater knowledge of costs and how these affected performance. The FMI aims of cost reduction and achievement of value-for-money have required the introduction of computerized management accounting and information systems so that managers can better control their allocation of resources, and react quickly to changing circumstances. The introduction of improved IT services has thus been an integral part of the Government's initiative.

2.3.2 'Next Steps'

The Government's aim further to improve management in the Civil Service for greater efficiency, effectiveness and quality of services to the public, was stepped up in 1988 when it accepted the main recommendations of the Efficiency Unit report "Improving Management in Government: the Next Steps". The Next Steps initiative builds upon and extends improvements to management and IT systems made under the FMI, particularly within the Executive Agencies which are being set up to take charge of the service delivery functions of core Civil Service Departments. Part of this responsibility involves the production of annual reports and accounts.

2.3.3 Implementation of plans: budgeting

The budgeting process is a key influence on the successful implementation of strategic and tactical plans at operational level. It is the means of delegating control and monitoring performance against predefined targets; it is paramount that budgets are effectively integrated within the organizational structure and that managerial responsibility and accountability is matched and communicated in an efficient way.

IT has played, and is continuing to play, a vital role in providing management in both the private and public sectors with the means to achieve their budgetary objectives. As budgeting is linked to profitability, it must be recognized that decisions about investment in IT Services and the integrated management accounting function can help provide the competitive edge necessary for survival of an organization.

2.3.4 PES/estimates

The Public Expenditure Survey (PES) is the Government's annual round of negotiations between the Treasury and Departments covering expenditure plans and programmes. PES initiates reviews of public expenditure:

* over the past five years

* over the current year

* plans for the next three years.

PES is also the basis for the Supply Estimates (the way Government allocates, monitors and controls net cash expenditure in-year). Clearly, it is important for the potential supplier of any service to Government to understand the expectations and the constraints these procedures have on the decision making capacity of public sector management.

Key features include:

* annual Cash Limits (which affect the purchasing decisions of the public spending organizations simply because of the annuality discipline)

* emphasis on the need to obtain value-for money rather than volumes of services.

The introduction and development of Computerized Management Accounting and Information Systems is a vital means of managing and controlling resources in a cost effective manner.

2.3.5 Investment Appraisal

Techniques of appraisal have been developed mainly in the context of decisions on capital spending, but the general principles apply to any proposal for spending or saving money that involves changes in the use of resources. Systematic appraisal entails:

* being clear about objectives

* thinking about different ways of meeting them

* estimating and presenting the costs and benefits of each potentially worthwhile option.

Used properly, appraisal leads to better decisions by policy makers and managers; it encourages both groups of people to question and justify what they do. And, it provides a framework for rational thought about the use of limited resources.

Investment Appraisal(IA) has long been recognized as an essential prerequisite to sound financial management both in the public and private sectors. The importance of IA has grown in recent years as an aid to decision making in its broadest sense, as a means of identifying efficiency savings and controlling investment expenditure to maximum effectiveness. There is often a trade-off between capital investment and running cost expenditure: ie between maximizing effectiveness in the long-term and the risk of failing to achieve short-term goals. Capital investment decisions are essentially longer-term decisions, and thus it is more difficult to hold management responsible and accountable for such decisions. Because the performance of a manager is often measured on the efficient and effective use of in-year allocated resources, there are only limited ways of holding managers responsible for investment decisions: this is why sound IA procedures are essential to good financial management.

The purchase of IT equipment and software is one of the most important investment decisions an organization must make. It is therefore crucial that such decisions are properly included in the organization's strategic planning. In the public sector there is a requirement for Departments to prepare and update an IS Strategy; thus IT managers both at the strategic and operational levels have a central role in helping to achieve organizational aims and objectives.

From the viewpoint of the business manager, IT investment and the supply of computer services is the same as any other planned expenditure or allocation of resource in that its utility is measured in its contribution to the effective, efficient and economic achievement of organizational goals.

2.4 Related guidance

This book is one of a series of modules issued as part of the CCTA IT Infrastructure Library. Although this module can be read in isolation, it should be used in conjunction with other IT Infrastructure Library modules.

The following modules in particular are closely related to cost management and should be referred to for further information. The overall framework of the costs and charges infrastructure pertaining to senior management is discussed in the **Planning and Control** module.

2.4.1 Service level management

Service level management is the process of managing the quality of delivered IT service in the face of changing business needs/customer requirements, according to a written Service Level Agreement (SLA). The SLA specifies customer expectations and IT services obligations. The Cost Manager will liaise about the pricing policies for the organization, their effects on customers and how the policies are expected to influence user behaviour. The more the SLA allows individual customers to request variations to service levels, the greater is the scope for (and potential benefits of) charging for IT services.

2.4.2 Capacity management

Capacity management is concerned with the provision and management of IT capacity to ensure required service levels can be achieved. It will be important to establish lines of communication with the Capacity Manager so that costs of equipment, workload processes and so on can be identified; the Capacity Manager will also use cost information to cost improvements to the system or changes to service levels.

2.4.3 Configuration management

Configuration management is the control of the components of hardware, software and documentation that make up the IT infrastructure. Configuration management specifies, identifies and controls changes to all components of the infrastructure: the use of configuration management as a data repository (including cost data) simplifies the collection of historical information and costs. In addition, configuration management facilitates auditing.

2.5 Standards

ISO 9000 series, EN29000 and BS5750 - Quality Management and Quality Assurance Standards

The Infrastructure Library codes of practice are designed to assist its adherents to obtain third-party quality certification to ISO 9001. Organizations' IT Directorates may wish to be so certified: CCTA will in future recommend that Facilities Management providers are certified.

3. Planning for cost management

3.0 Understanding and planning for cost management

This section covers the evaluation and planning activities necessary to prepare for the implementation of a proper cost management system within IT infrastructure management.

The first step is to initiate a cost management project and appoint the Project Team members. The appointed Cost Manager must be a prominent member of the team.

It is recommended that all of the work necessary for the design of a cost management system is managed according to the PRINCE (PRojects IN Controlled Environments) method.

Essentially, use of PRINCE divides the work into two separate projects:

* feasibility study

* development (which includes systems analysis and design) and implementation.

A Project Board should be created to oversee the Project. The purpose of the Project Board will be to provide overall guidance and advice to the Project Team and to monitor the Project. The board should comprise the following personnel:

* Executive - the director of IS in the organization

* Senior User - either a senior manager in the Financial Services division or one of the users to be invoiced

* Senior Technical - a suitable candidate would be the IT Services Manager.

The project board must appoint a project manager, to manage all aspects of the work and to act as a contact for progress reports, feasibility reports and so on. The project board and the project manager will jointly decide on the personnel required for the Project Team. A Cost Manager will of course be the most important appointment. The Cost Manager will be the chief architect of the cost management system. A job description for the Cost Manager is in Annex B.9.

The board will make all of their business decisions based on the recommendations of the project team's feasibility study and will set appropriate budgets for the development and implementation project.

The project team

It is vital that the team has a fundamental appreciation of both the organization's business and the IT Services section in order to understand the options available to management. Team members must understand the principles of cost management and sections 3.0.1 - 3.0.3 are intended to provide the proper context and background for the work.

Project manager

The project manager has overall responsibility for managing the project from feasibility to implementation. The project manager will, amongst other things, be responsible for:

* setting of quality objectives

* verification of plans

* agreement of performance indicators

* definition of responsibilities for the team

* preparation of Project and Stage level plans

* setting objectives for the stage managers

* scheduling and monitoring of control points

* creation of a configuration management structure for the cost management system (see the IT Infrastructure Library module **Configuration Management** for guidance) probably in collaboration with the Capacity Manager and/or Configuration Manager

* preparation of periodic highlight reports

* presentations at mid-stage and end-stage assessment meetings

* enforcement of technical exception procedures

* preparation of exception plans.

3.0.1 Understanding the issues

The provision of IT services to users depends on two major factors:

* capacity

* cost.

There is a tension between these factors; improving the quality of services may increase costs because it is necessary to increase capacity. Similarly, cutting costs may alter capacity requirements and the quality and variety of services provided. It is the balance of the tension between costs and capacity that must be maintained if services are to be provided which are:

* of good quality

* matched to business need

* economic.

Identifying all of the costs necessary to provide IT services and establishing a fair means of charging for those services places IT service provision on a business-like footing. Customers are aware that they pay a fair price for their use of IT services and because of the charges, do not view the resources as a commodity which can be wasted. It is the responsibility of all IT Services Managers to establish the true cost of providing IT services and to consider charging for the services: above all else, adopting the principles of cost management will establish the IT Services section as a business oriented and cost conscious organization.

3.0.2 Costing data classification

Costs should be classified as either capital or revenue. For budgetary control purposes and for the production of annual accounts it is necessary to identify and ring-fence capital and revenue expenditure. Capital costs are typically the purchase or major enhancement of fixed assets, for example computer equipment (building and plant) and software packages. It is important to remember that it is not always the actual cost of items purchased during the year that is included in the calculation of the cost of the services, but the depreciation and interest charge for the year. The day-to-day costs of running the IT Services section ie staff costs, hardware maintenance, electricity etc, represent revenue expenditure.

After classification, costs must all be allocated to standard cost units. The number and types of cost units differ from installation to installation due to size, the organizational structure and services required. The cost units need to be discrete and set up in such a way as to enable costs to be easily attributed to each unit. Shared costs such as central administration must be apportioned across the various cost units - see Annex D.

Costing and charging

Costing and charging are integral parts of IT infrastructure management accounting techniques. They are different but linked sets of activities. Costing involves identifying and accounting for the costs of running the IT directorate and providing the services. Charging is the process by which the costs are recovered. A charge is the price paid by users of the service.

The difference between costing and charging has to be **clearly** understood, and the responsibility for each has to be defined. Costing and charging must be regarded as separate functions (accounts payable and accounts receivable). The differences are made clear in this section of the module.

Both costing and charging are concerned with managing the IT infrastructure and providing a professional interface to the users of IT. Figure 2 outlines some of the more important aspects of costing and charging.

The most visible and politically important of the functions, that of **charging**, is concerned with the recovery of IT services expenditures in a fair and equitable way, related to how services are used. **Costing** is concerned with providing detailed information on where and for what reason money is spent within IT Services.

	Costing	Charging
Planning (annually)	Establish standard unit costs for each major IT service resource	Establish a pricing portfolio and a "price list" for each item to be used in calculating the charge
Operations (eg monthly)	Monitor expenditures and compare plans to actuals by cost unit	Compile and issue invoices
Figure 2: Costing and charging for IT services		

There are two distinct phases associated with costing and charging:

* **planning** phase (annual) where cost projections and workload forecasting form a basis for unit cost calculations and price setting

* **operational** phase to verify that cost management is going according to plan and to take action to address problems, issue invoices and collect the income.

Planning and follow-up activities for the two functions must be carried out in an integrated fashion.

With this structure in mind the steps to be carried out are as follows:

* establish and agree the organizational and budget boundaries of IT Services

* develop a spreadsheet to capture the projected expenditures allocated to projected usage of major resource types, to establish the cost of carrying out the work of the IT Services section (see also Annex D)

* establish the unit prices for the calculation of charges

* develop a feed-back system to verify that the actual expenditure and usage are, within acceptable limits, comparable with cost and workload projections

* ensure the mechanisms for changing resource allocation or charges (if it becomes necessary to correct mismatches) are in place

* examine the cost of maintaining existing quality levels and how much the organization loses through waste, not getting something right, or through poor implementation.

The analysis related to the planning activities should be carried out using spreadsheets or PC packages. The analysis of the follow-up data is best carried out with the assistance of a proprietary accounting package or a similar product which may have been produced by the organization.

3.0.3 Management options

Management can choose to operate IT Services, *inter alia*, to make profits or to break even. If the former, the organization can adopt the Computer Services Business Centre (CSBC) approach; if the latter, accountability can be demonstrated by the production of Memorandum Trading Accounts (MTA).

*Memorandum Trading
Account (MTA)*

MTAs are informal working documents and do not necessarily include a Balance Sheet. They are designed to show first the forecast figures used to determine the level of fees and charges for a repayment service, and subsequently the outturn figures to provide a record of performance.

These accounts will include both cash and non-cash costs which, in effect, identify the full economic cost of running the business. MTAs are not published or formally audited by the Comptroller and Auditor General (C&AG).

The benefits of producing an MTA include improved cost control over service provision and consistency in approach by different organizations.

*Computer Services
Business Centre (CSBC)*

A CSBC is (in the context of this module) a method of managing the IT Services section where it has sufficient autonomy to operate as a separate business entity, but with business objectives set by the organization. Figure 3 shows the relationship between the CSBC and the users of the IT services.

Figure 3 illustrates the relationship between the customer demands for computer services and the CSBC supply of resources. The system described is customer oriented: it starts from the position that CSBC products should be aimed to satisfy customer requirements at minimum cost; thus the CSBC should be demand driven. However, it is also recognized that the size and scope of the CSBC, any policy constraints and the pricing strategy, will also have an impact upon resource availability.

A CSBC can be created with the business objective of making a profit, breaking even or operating with a subsidy. The key characteristics are that:

* deliverables or products are clearly identified and sold into a marketplace

* each product or service carries a price tag.

The IT Services section must be assumed to pay for its own upkeep, probably with some financial support for capital expenditures. Choosing to operate as a CSBC is usually the first step along the path to a truly commercial IT Services section, one in which the users (customers) have some freedom of choice to go elsewhere if they are not satisfied with the quality and/or price. The CSBC approach provides the IT Services section with a certain amount of autonomy, but it also imposes responsibilities.

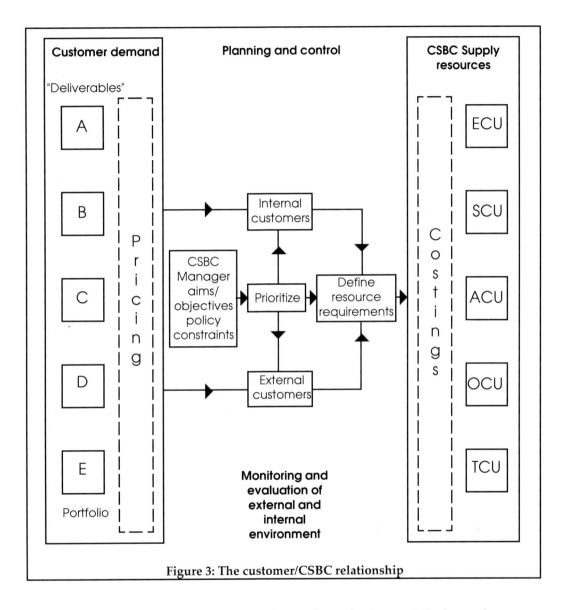

Figure 3: The customer/CSBC relationship

Utility Cost Centre (UCC)   A UCC is distinct from a business unit in that performance is not measured in terms of projected or anticipated rate of return but on how efficiently and effectively the UCC functions in respect of the services it provides to users.

3.1 Procedures

The feasibility study can begin once the Project Team has obtained a satisfactory knowledge of the principles of cost management presented in section 3.0.

The following paragraphs describe how to plan for cost management. They describe the use of a feasibility study (to identify the usefulness of implementing cost management) and discuss the systems analysis and design considerations required for a cost management function within an IT Services organization.

3.1.1 Feasibility study

The Terms of Reference (TOR) will set the objectives of the feasibility study. Decisions about the full study will be based on the fact finding carried out during the feasibility study, although decisions may be imposed because of management adoption of CSBC, MTA or UCC approaches. A sample TOR is provided in Annex B. The following items should be considered for inclusion in the TOR:

* the organization's management requirements (what cost management is intended to achieve, whether to opt for cost recovery or profits)

* evaluation and quantification of the likely benefits to be accrued from the introduction of cost management

* the resources, staff and costs needed to introduce and run cost management (project costs and ongoing costs)

* identification of cost management activities already being carried out within the IT Directorate

* evaluation of any support tools (eg monitoring, accounting) that are already available, or can be obtained

* specification of the financial interfaces to the rest of the organization - do users have meaningful budgets for non-IT expenditure, are they simply for information purposes, or do budgets not exist?

* assessment of scope for integration of invoicing and purchasing systems (if applicable in your organization) to the costing system, so that purchase data does not have to be re-input

* the deliverables required of a cost management function

* the likely business components (for example, cheques, enquiries, pay-slips)

* identification of the information needed for the cost management function and whether it is, or can be, made available

* any risk areas that might militate against successful introduction of cost management

* performance indicators

* number of users

* the management view on maintaining application development costs as a separate account and whether those costs should be charged to users or to the application developers

* specification of how a new cost management system will interface with any existing system or systems.

It is not possible to give prescriptive guidance on the business components to choose in each circumstance. It is important for the project team to gain a clear understanding of the business of the organization and highlight areas of doubt for a senior management decision (for example two users may share the responsibility for the production of a payroll slip - who should be invoiced?). Many business components support several user departments in the organization: be aware that negotiations are needed to establish **who** pays the bills!

Once the feasibility study has been carried out, a report must be produced, identifying and justifying the feasible solutions and seeking management approval to proceed to the next stages of the project.

When management approval has been given, a project plan must be produced for the development and implementation phase (this stage can be regarded as part of the feasibility study).

The project plan must cover the:

* systems analysis phase (sections 3.1.2-3.1.14 and Annex D)

* design phase (Annex E)

     *   development and implementation phase (section 4)

     *   post-implementation phase (section 5).

3.1.2 Initiate systems analysis

The second project begins with the systems analysis necessary to develop and design the proposed cost management system. It is recommended that Structured Systems Analysis and Design Method (SSADM) is used for systems analysis.

The following sections (3.1.3-3.1.14) cover the main tasks to be completed during the systems analysis phase of the development project.

3.1.3 Mount a cost awareness campaign

Mounting a cost awareness campaign in the organization prior to project initiation will have significant benefits. User personnel could be given short presentations about identifying costs and why costs must be controlled. These presentations should take place after the acceptance of the feasibility study and just prior to the analysis and design phase. Cost awareness campaigns gain commitment because staff appreciate being kept informed about new developments.

The presentation should include guidance about when cost management is to be implemented and in Government organizations, explain the need to align cost management plans to PES and Budget estimates.

The presentation must cover plans for cost recovery and the timescale over which it is intended to recover the identified costs. If it is the policy of the organization to profit from IT, or indeed to plough back profit into IT, then some information about how the profits are to be used is also appropriate.

3.1.4 The planning cycle

It is important to analyze the planning cycles in the organization so that the required plans are identified and made available to the Project Team.

Both business and IT Directorates are expected to produce plans (which should be consistent with supply estimates) which are to be subsumed into the IT Tactical plan (ie workload and resource forecasts). Production of these plans is iterative and the Project Team should be aware of the details of their production (timing and content). In Government such plans are produced within the framework of supply estimates and public expenditure surveys (PES).

The overall budgets are available from business and IT tactical plans (these plans should of course be consistent with supply estimates) and the data must be fed into the IT cost plan and IT cost recovery plan. IT cost monitoring and IT cost recovery monitoring are performed against these plans. Clearly the monitoring processes must feed back into the iterative plans produced by the business and the IT Directorate.

3.1.5 Estimate costs

Annex D provides more detailed information about estimating costs and monitoring costs.

Expressed very simply, the process begins by identifying the IT services that will need to be provided for the coming financial year, then estimating the total cost of resources needed to provide these services. The cost of these resources is then broken down into costs per unit of output. The costs per unit of the various resources are built up to provide estimated costs per individual service.

The data necessary to identify **costs** is generally readily available in most IT service centres. It is necessary to know, for each user, the proportionate use of the following:

* staff

* accommodation

* equipment (hardware)

* software costs.

Total costs therefore must be broken down, in order to allocate the correct proportions to the individual users.

If costs are not properly identified it is likely that the initial rate calculations will be shown to be inaccurate during the monitoring periods. It is possible - and recommended - to revise the projections (and charges, if necessary) during pilot study periods or when Service Level Agreements (SLA) are revised.

To paint a more complete picture of cost estimates, the Project Team must attempt to quantify the anticipated growth (or other change) in workloads expected in each financial year. This information might be present in the SLA, may be obtained from the Capacity Manager or from the User community. Workload information is necessary to establish the amount of work, by business units, (ie the chargeable units which are discussed later in this section) which is processed by the IT Services section and from this, calculate the unit costs for the coming years for each cost unit.

3.1.6 Monitor costs

Generally, there are five major cost units associated with IT cost classification:

* Equipment (ECU)

* Software (SCU)

* Organization (OCU)

* Accommodation (ACU)

* Transfer (TCU).

An organization may well identify other costs units: this is perfectly acceptable so long as the components of each cost unit are clearly defined.

Some examples of items to be monitored within these classifications include:

* mainframes (ECU)

* maintenance and support (SCU)

* cost of software (SCU)

* staff (OCU)

* furniture (ACU)

* work performed by a user on behalf of another user (TCU)

* quality (all).

The identified costs are monitored regularly every month if possible in the first year and thereafter at regular intervals appropriate to the organization once the costing system is established.

The information is essential for forward financial planning and capacity planning. For example, it is possible that a particular customer is utilizing resources at a higher rate than was anticipated: in this instance the IT Directorate may wish to dampen (or restrict) the demands of the user, possibly by increasing the charges.

Ideally, monitoring should be automatic, using one or more software tools (section 7 provides guidance on choosing tools).

3.1.7 Pricing of computer services

The pricing of any product or service is often a complex issue involving:

* the determination of a pricing objective

* direct and indirect costs

* what the market will bear

* the perceived demand of the commodity

* the number of potential customers and competition.

To calculate the charge for providing IT services internally, or between (or to) subsidiaries, an organization must decide what it is hoping to achieve prior to implementation. One key factor will be to analyze the motivational aspects of charging, considering both the effects upon the provider and the user of the service. The objective is to optimize the behaviour of both parties in achieving the organization's aims.

3.1.7.1 Pricing

Pricing is one element of the marketing adage - "product, pricing, promotion, place". Deciding upon the appropriate charge/price is, therefore, not merely a question of cost recovery but also of its leading impact upon the demand for the product. Managers' short and longer-term expectations of the commodity's utility concerning the market place may well, therefore, require the Cost Manager to develop a flexible strategy to fit particular circumstances over time.

The maximization of profit and/or achieving an anticipated rate of return will no doubt figure greatly in managers' considerations. For the IT Services Manager selling services to user departments, the price to be charged may be based on the market rate negotiated down to take account of any administrative cost savings resulting from the contract. Whatever pricing decision is taken it will be essential for the IT Services Manager to ascertain the standard costs of providing the service.

Examples of other pricing methods include:

* cost plus

* marginal cost plus

* opportunity cost

* going rate

* what the market will bear

* negotiated contract price

* target return.

Some of these options are self-explanatory (what the market will bear and negotiated contract price) - the others are defined below.

3.1.7.2 Alternative pricing methods

Cost plus

There are a number of cost plus pricing models. The basic form is:

price = cost + % mark up

The cost can be defined in several ways as can the mark up, for example:

* full cost (including profit margin)

* marginal cost + mark up (sufficient to cover average fixed costs, costs per unit and profit/return on capital, if required).

Going rate

Where the price charged is an average of, or the same as, prices charged by other members of the **same** industry.

Target return

Total cost plus mark up to reflect a required return on the assets used in provision of the service.

3.1.7.3 Pricing portfolio

A CSBC may determine that it can produce certain deliverables at lower cost if there is greater demand. The CSBC Manager may then decide to offer differentiated prices depending upon the quantity/volume of the service demanded. The pricing policy may be reflected in the service level contract prices negotiated between the customer and the CSBC Manager.

Pricing deliverables over a life-cycle

The CSBC Manager may wish to consider the duration of a customer requirement for IT services and seek regular updated forecasts if demand is likely to change. This may be particularly important if there are peaks and troughs in customer demand especially when these are not synchronized to the availability of CSBC resource capacity. It may be that the CSBC Manager should consider setting specific prices for particular times of usage; but this will depend upon size, circumstance, and objectives of the CSBC.

3.1.8 Charging policies

The charging policy to be employed may be based on one of the following.

Communication of information

Charging information is passed to user managers to make them aware of the cost of the resources used by their business. Do this by:

* calculating and circulating to managers details of actual business unit costs

* as above, but including details about how much the IT Services Directorate would charge, should a charge-back system be operated.

Pricing flexibility

The CSBC Manager may wish to set prices for an annual period; however, where new resource requirements are committed to meet the needs of particular customers it may be necessary to build into any contract for the provision of such services an escalation clause to reduce the risk of excess capacity usage, particularly where there is opportunity to sell surplus capacity to other potential customers.

Notional charging

Charging for IT services against notional budgets is useful when a charge-back system is being introduced for the first time. Notional charging allows the IT Services section to gain experience and time to correct errors in the charging formulae or cost recovery plans and familiarizes customers with the concept of being charged for using IT resources.

Notional charging is not recommended for long-term use unless the organization does not intend to move to a real charging system, because the incentive to become cost conscious is lessened when money does not change hands.

3.1.8.1 Factors governing choice of policies

Four factors govern the requirements of a charging system in the organization. For example, full commercial charging requires that costs can be forecast and a set of charging units selected that are predictable, measurable and understandable by the user. The four factors are as follows.

Full recovery of all expenditures

If the IT Directorate opts for full recovery of all costs, then it is opting to function as an autonomous unit, financially self-sufficient. This then requires that costs can be forecast and a charging system selected that is rational, easily understood and very accurate (although not necessarily based on business unit charging).

Shape user behaviour

Shaping user behaviour has two aspects:

* to avoid expensive system components being misused or overused

* to shift potential work to off-peak periods.

The first requires that cost management identifies unit costs by equipment class, and that differential charging is selected.

Establishing a pricing policy helps shape user behaviour and flexibility to adapt to changes in a competitive environment.

Recovery according to usage

Recovering costs according to usage requires that the selected charging units have a reasonable correlation with the amount of resources required to process the work, thereby promoting the perception of a fair pricing and charging structure.

Market-priced services

Introducing market-priced services requires an efficient and effective IT infrastructure management with capacity properly managed, costs well controlled, and services delivered according to expectations.

Pitching services at market price in turn leads to being able to provide quality services consistently, and at reasonable prices, thereby establishing a professional interface with customers. Ideally, the charging will be based on business units as used by the customers.

3.1.8.2 Summary

Four specific objectives must be incorporated into the requirements of a charging system and these must be fulfilled if the system is to function properly:

* chargeable items must be understood by the user, with reasonable correlation to usage of resources, including hardware, software, accommodation, and organization

* cost management must be set in place to provide details on, and justification for, expenditure

* service level management must be set in place to provide information on the impact of discounting and surcharging, and of differential charging (and also to help to ensure delivery of service in accordance with user expectations)

* IT infrastructure management should be set in place to ensure well-balanced systems where good IT services are provided at reasonable costs.

3.1.9 Reasons for charging

In the context of an internal IT Services section, one of the reasons for charging is to make both customers and IT service providers aware of the costs of the services which are being provided. A consequence of this should be more efficient use of IT resources and good matching of usage to business needs. The implications and advantages of charging vary depending on what freedom the customers of the IT Services section have to go elsewhere for their IT needs. Clearly, charging will have greater impact where customers have the discretion to go elsewhere. But even when they must use internal IT services, charging continues to bring the benefit of greater cost awareness.

3.1.10 Users tied to internal IT services

In many IT organizations, users are tied to using the internal IT services. This situation usually progresses through varying stages, typically:

* tied, services provided "free"

* tied, notional charging introduced

* tied, actual charges introduced (sometimes subsidized, initially)

* untied, real charging.

Where no direct charge is levied, customers do not take account of the cost of producing a service and tend to treat it as a free good. As a consequence they may be extravagant and uneconomical in their use of IT services.

The existence of different charges for different services enables users to decide on priorities between services, (based on the relative cost of providing them). Similarly, the use of differential charging (peak/off peak or batch/on-line usage) encourages helpful changes in customer behaviour, often at relatively little cost to IT Services in terms of the perceived service. For instance, the smoothing out of daily demand for processing capacity reduces the overall capacity required for a given set of users.

3.1.11 Untied situation

In an untied situation charging becomes particularly important because it enables customers to choose between using the in-house IT Services section or outside suppliers, based on the relative quality and price of services offered.

If IT provision is to be untied (ie users can buy in from other sources), the IT providers should operate on a commercial basis with the aim of recovering full cost, including return on capital employed. When users are first freed from being tied to internal IT services, it is not uncommon to find some organizations subsidizing the cost of the internal IT services, to discourage users from switching suppliers. In practice, subsidizing IT services should be discouraged, since prices will appear to be unrealistically low.

Charging at full cost entails recovering all revenue spend costs associated with providing an IT service (including a share of overheads), insurance premium, depreciation of fixed assets and interest on capital employed. It is important that the charge for each service provided by an IT Services section should, wherever possible, be charged out at full cost, thus avoiding the problem of cross-subsidization between services.

Cross-subsidization between different customers of the same service is to be avoided whenever practicable. Where, exceptionally, surpluses and deficits accumulated by a number of services are pooled so that they break-even in total, the effect is to subsidize the cost of one service by the income of another. Such cross-subsidies may lead to a department being criticized for taxing one group of customers for the benefit of another group.

An IT Services section might not charge out a particular service at full cost when:

*   it is possible to distinguish between internal and external customers, where the internal users are the ones with the primary reason for establishing the IT Services section in the first place and external users are secondary. In this case the external users could be charged a premium rate in order to make a profit

*   there is standby capacity set aside for certain customers which can be used on a short-term basis by others at marginal cost.

See also section 5 of this module (Post-implementation).

3.1.12 Conditions for charging to be effective

In considering whether it is worth investing time and resources in setting up a charging system, regard should be given as to whether customers:

*   have meaningful budgets in which internal IT Services charges are regarded as real costs to be set against other items in the budget. If this is not the case, many of the advantages of charging are reduced; though it is still worthwhile doing the costing to provide cost data as management information

*   have an element of choice in their level of usage of the IT Services section's services, both overall and at particular times.

If demand is not sensitive to pricing, charging is effective only as a mechanism for funding IT service provision: alternative arrangements such as inter-departmental reviews must take place to verify and assure the cost effectiveness of IT service provision (see also section 5).

Any considerations, however, must take into account the fact that customers perception of IT is constantly changing and that they expect an ever increasing business-like relationship.

3.1.13 Decide your chargeable items

The sole item directly under control of charging is the one relating to chargeable items. Chargeable items should relate to the user in a way that can be understood and controlled so that, at least theoretically, if the user needs to save money, processing can be stopped.

The obvious chargeable items are thus business units. Requirements are that the items must be identifiable, measurable and predictable.

The more closely the chargeable items relate to the organization's business deliverables the better the interface to the users. Only lack of information should force charging to be directly based on resource usage; this lack of information must be overcome and it is important that in the analysis phase, steps are taken to ensure the future availability of information.

Consider the following example: airlines sell air tickets; they do not issue an invoice covering usage of plane, fuel, food, proportional crew costs and so on. Air tickets are thus the logical chargeable item. Airport tax may be charged as a separate item; this is synonymous with the Transfer Cost Unit mentioned in Annex D, para 3.

Occasionally, business units are not suitable as chargeable items because they are not consistent with the resources consumed. In such cases, a more detailed charging structure has to be established for those particular services.

An example could be work performed by a statistical analysis program, which on one occasion may run through very quickly and on another, consume vast amounts of resource. Although over a period of time a business unit charge may collect the appropriate money owed for resources consumed, accurate charging for the resource-intensive runs may influence the customer to alter the way in which the program runs.

Often, business components are not easily measurable. In the past, programs were rarely written to produce logical business components: too often many users utilize portions of a multitude of programs, each of which contributes to the production of parts of many business components. Batch systems in particular are characterized by this trait. Standards should be established to ensure that programs are written which recognize the need for clear identification of business components.

Do bear in mind that the more freedom the customer has to define his own service, the more detailed the charging structure has to be.

3.1.14 Specify systems

Having considered the key issues involved in assessing IT costs and deciding the basis for IT charging, the project team should now be able to recommend the processes most suitable for cost management in their organization. These recommendations must form the systems specification.

3.1.15 Design

Once the project team has decided upon the system specification most suited to their organization, the detailed design can begin. Annex E of this module provides an outline of some of the design processes which have been recently used in commercial environments. The annex identifies tasks which are germane to the production of a detailed specification for the proposed system.

Testing of the design should be performed according to the guidelines in the IT Infrastructure Library module **Testing Software for Operational Use**.

3.1.16 Piloting the cost management system

If the cost management system is new or involves charging users for the first time, it is recommended that the first six months of running the system should be viewed as a pilot scheme. The pilot should be aimed at improving cost awareness.

It should begin at the start of the financial year, so that there is sufficient data available to specify targets or budgets for future expenditure.

If monitoring of the revised costs or charges identifies either huge rebates or the need to increase charges, then the credibility of the cost management process could be compromised. If this is identified during the pilot, the charging algorithms and/or the cost projections can be re-examined and corrected before introducing the system fully, thus maintaining credibility. See also Annex E.6 of this module.

Customers should be notified at the earliest possible stage about events that are likely to cause changes to their invoices.

It is important that customers are aware of any likely alterations to charges which may result from changes to:

* IT infrastructure

* IT organization

* other IT changes outside customer control.

In this way, adjustments will be viewed in the proper context of careful and meticulous management of IT costs.

3.1.17 Performance indicators

The obvious measures of the success of the cost management system are that:

* cost recovery profiles and expenditure profiles prove to be accurate

* charges, where applied, are seen to be fair

* the IT Directorate is provided with the expected income/level of profits.

The business objective of either break-even or profit, whichever is the objective of the organization, should therefore be met.

However, even the most accurately determined profiles may go awry because of changes in customer behaviour or perhaps changes in the customers' business resulting from changes in the behaviour of the clients. Whilst it is laudable to aim for accuracy in the calculations of the profiles, there are additional aspects of success which can be measured and used to determine the effectiveness of the cost management system. It is of course important that some measures of performance are set, in order to establish targets for the business. These measures may cover not only efficiency, effectiveness and economy but also the quality of the delivered services.

Examples of performance indicators which could be used include:

* plans and budgets produced on time

* specified reports produced at the required time

* the inventory schedules are kept up-to-date

* all costs are accounted for

* timeliness of annual audits

* meeting of monthly, quarterly and annual business objectives

* the number (and severity) of changes required to the cost management system

* accuracy of monthly, quarterly and annual profiles

* number of changes made to the charging algorithm (where appropriate).

3.2 Dependencies

The most important dependency is that there is senior management commitment to the introduction of a cost management system. Senior managers must be prepared to specify what they require from the cost management system and how the system will interface with other systems (eg capacity management) in the organization.

A fully functioning IT cost management system will also depend on the availability of detailed and accurate information. The project team must identify the:

* business objectives of the organization in introducing cost management to IT services

* alignment of the cost management system with the production of the IS strategic plan and the IT tactical plan

* information needed

* interfaces required to obtain the information

* format of introduction/data and the level of detail necessary

* cost of introducing cost management.

Professional accounting skills are required to help ensure the costing and charging systems are well designed. Where accountants are not otherwise available, approach auditors for advice.

3.2.1 Responsibilities

The cost management system functions best when clear boundaries have been agreed (ie which costs are applicable directly to the IT budget) and clearly identifiable deliverables have been chosen.

Responsibility for costing and charging for IT services belongs to the IT Services section, since it is their task to ensure that the business objectives underpinned by IT are met; responsibility for cost management of IT services cannot be placed anywhere else.

3.2.2 Tools

Except for very small IT Services sections, it is not practical to attempt cost management without the availability of a software tool. Tools are discussed in section 7 of this module. Report production facilities are also a fundamental prerequisite.

3.3 People

3.3.1 Staffing

The Cost Manager is responsible for the day-to-day operation of the costing and charging systems and ensuring that the planned structure is operational. Overall control should be vested in the IT Services Manager who is ultimately responsible for IT service costs. Staff issues are discussed in section 3.0.

3.3.2 Organization

Cost management is an integral part of the IT Services management structure and must be permanently staffed. The IT Services Manager is responsible for the cost management function and the Cost Manager must report directly to the IT Services Manager.

3.3.3 Training

Everyone involved with cost management should be provided with appropriate training about IT cost accounting. It is also recommended that they understand the fundamentals of capacity, change, configuration and service level management issues.

3.3.4 IT Directorate management

The IT Services section must ensure that its cost management system conforms to auditing and other relevant rules and standards laid down by the organization.

3.4   Timing

It is important to plan the expenditure and cost recovery profiles annually. The plans should cover each month in the financial year to facilitate monthly monitoring and cover peaks and troughs. Actual expenditures and recoveries are monitored and compared at the end of each month: the expenditures and recoveries are also compared with what was planned. It is also appropriate to plan changes to the cost management system to coincide with SLA reviews and any change should be reflected in the SLAs.

The planning phase can be expected to take 3-6 months, mostly dependent on the size and complexity of the IT Services section and the availability of data. This planning phase is used for the collection of statistics which will be useful in system testing (see 4.1.6).

The preparation for cost management can be carried out at any time, but it is recommended that any new or amended cost management system is brought into use at the start of a new financial year. See also section 4.

4. Implementation

The following section describes the final development, testing and implementation of the planned cost management system.

4.1 Procedures

4.1.1 Documentation

Towards the conclusion of the analysis and design phase, document the operational procedures covering normal daily, weekly, monthly and yearly operation of all the aspects of cost management, including the planning, cost reporting, cost recovery reporting and billing activities. In addition to the documents covering the IT operational procedures, develop user manuals covering learning, references and user guide for the Cost Manager and his staff.

To attempt to implement a system without proper and complete documentation to help the customers and support personnel and to complement training, is inadvisable, particularly when the system involves accounts procedures which are most probably alien to each of the affected sub-cultures in the organization. The complexity of the support documentation varies depending on whether the user is the cost management team, Help Desk or a business customer.

It is not possible to provide specific guidance on these issues because the costing (and charging) systems design varies from one organization to another, depending on their exact need. However, it is vital to cover how:

* IT management and customer management are informed about progress

* costing data is to be collected

* costs are monitored

* the charging (if appropriate) system works and what pricing structures are to be used

* accounts are to be settled

* responsibilities are allocated for policing the cost management system and producing reports, invoices, and so on

* (and when) auditing takes place

    * contingency option(s) work (see this section of the module and Annex E)

    * error reporting is handled

    * change control is applied to the cost management system.

If, as is recommended, SSADM was used in the analysis and design phases of the project, circulate the documented SSADM deliverables so that members of the IT Directorate and users can appreciate the flow of information in the costing system.

4.1.2 Code the designed components

Once the system components are identified it is important that the coding reflects how the information is to be used. For example mainframe/ network applications should be used to collect Business Unit information. If the Cost Units described in this module are used, be certain that the data required for each Cost Unit can be identified and collated.

Cost management is based on the annual cycle of cost data collection; coding should thus be relatively simple. For this reason it is unusual to decide upon a mainframe application as the means of implementing the system. Unless the organization is very large, it is recommended that the design should be implemented on a PC.

4.1.3 Set up data recording

In parallel with implementing the system design, examine the existing data recording mechanisms for information about planning, reporting and (eventually) charging. Information will be needed about:

    * workloads

    * services

    * costs

    * resource inventories (hardware and software).

Annex D provides more information about this subject.

Workload and service data should be available from the capacity management database (CMDB): cost information (including future acquisitions) should be available from accounts departments; or, where configuration management is practised, from the Configuration Manager. The Configuration Manager should also be capable of providing inventories of all resources.

The data recording task does not end once the initial data is available. Cost management is based on an annual cycle and it is important to ensure that all required data is made available on time, every time. It is not possible to perform accurate monitoring unless the required data is routinely available.

4.1.4 Install and test software tools

Where software tools have been developed or purchased, install and test them at this stage to ensure that they function as expected. See the IT Infrastructure Library module **Testing Software for Operational Use**.

4.1.5 Completion of worksheets

The example worksheets provided in Annexes D and E can be used as the basis for the design of reports for management.

The worksheets are appropriate to a manual system, or can be used as the basis for electronic spreadsheet design. Some packages are available which use these designs.

4.1.6 Monitoring

Arrange monitoring procedures for measuring actual resources consumed (regardless of whether a charging system is to be introduced) three to six months in advance of system implementation in order to gain experience of monitoring. This data is essential for forward financial planning and capacity management. See also 3.1.16.

4.1.7 Implementation

Produce detailed implementation schedule

Create a detailed step-by-step schedule covering the activities needed to take the project through to post implementation. The schedule covers the activities and the sign off criteria for each phase, the manpower involved and the timescales to be met. The schedule should also contain information on what to do if the phases cannot be implemented according to plan.

Contingency planning

It is possible that the contingency plan is to withdraw the cost management system entirely - this is probably the sole option when monitoring reveals that cost recovery plans are completely awry, and this is not discovered until the cost management system is in full use. In this case, management approval is needed to start again, probably from the beginning of the systems analysis stage to identify the cause(s) of the discrepancies.

When considering the implementation of the cost management project, it is recommended that arrangements are made for the maintenance of essential manual records and what is to be done in the event of major problems.

A properly designed system providing timely recognition of costs to senior management soon becomes indispensable. Simply holding manual data may not satisfy those who come to rely on such a cost management system. The project team should therefore identify what is mandatory and what is desirable from a contingency system. Review the way in which the system is being used so that the manual system is providing the appropriate data. See also 5.1.5, Annexes D and E, and the IT Infrastructure Library **Contingency Planning** module.

Sign-off

Write a report for management outlining the state of the system at the termination of the implementation phase. Once the report has been accepted by management, the project can be signed off.

The report should include a statement about why the project was instituted and what it achieved. How much the project cost and the expected running costs should also be included. Provide metrics about how costs were identified in the past and how this has changed. Describe also any benefits and problems in the new system. If possible describe any obvious savings which have been made possible through implementation of cost management principles.

4.2 Dependencies

The fundamental dependency for implementation is that the costing and charging structure developed during the planning stage is fully understood by everybody involved and fully supported by IT Services management.

Clearly there is also a dependency on the information from all sources being available in order to perform the cost management tasks.

The dependencies listed in section 3.2 are also relevant to implementation.

4.3   People

See section 3.3.

4.4   Timing

The timing estimated for the implementation phase is approximately 6 months, depending on tools and information availability. Align the implementation of a costing and charging system with the start of the financial year and allow a substantial period for system testing and parallel running - 3 months is ideal.

5. Post-implementation and audit

5.1 Procedures

This section concerns the post-implementation review of the cost management project and the procedures for the ongoing operation of the cost management system. This section also covers:

* reviews for efficiency, effectiveness and economy

* auditing for conformance to laid down procedures

* dealing with variance from forecast.

5.1.1 Post-implementation review

As soon as is practical following implementation of the cost management project (about three months would be ideal) instigate a review to assess:

* how well the project was managed

* adherence to timescale and budget

* lessons to be learned (both for the future of cost management and for other IT projects).

A formal post-implementation review represents the final phase of the development project; both successes and shortcomings are objectively assessed. The post-implementation reviewers and subsequent periodic reviewers of the cost management system check that it is working effectively and that the Cost Manager is keeping the system under continual review (and that all identified deficiencies are corrected at source to prevent recurrence). The objective of the review is to ensure that the characteristics of an effective cost management system are clearly identifiable, viz:

* cost projections (overall and for each business supported) are accurate each month and at the year end

* standard unit costs are on target (Annex D)

* business unit costs are as predicted (Annex D)

* all costs, including unexpected costs, are accounted for

* personnel related cost information is accurate and up-to-date

* accommodation and environment costs are accurate and up-to-date

* interfaces to capacity management and service level management are working and provide the necessary workload information

* the interface to configuration management provides regular hardware/software data updates

* specified reports are produced on time (including reports about how user budgets are being spent on IT).

Note that the accuracy of predictions and projections listed above may be compromised by matters outside the control of the Cost Manager. Where predictions are affected inform the appropriate manager(s) and ensure that steps are being taken to correct the offending system(s). See also 5.1.3.

Where charging is in place, the characteristics of an effective charging system should also be clearly identifiable and these include:

* interfaces to capacity, service level and configuration management as previously described

* invoices are issued on time

* income is collected on time

* price lists are available on time and are accurate

* any changes to the charges/price lists are implemented within target timescales.

Other items to be included in the review are general indicators of the success of the project and apply equally to costing and to charging. These include:

* user satisfaction - charges are considered fair, the cost management system is understood and users are satisfied with the manner in which it operates

* customers are neither under-charged nor over-charged for their IT services (this is in terms of correctness according to price lists and justice, in that discrepancies in costs/charges are identified quickly and without affecting customers)

* the IT Services business objectives, that the cost management system directly supports, are met monthly, quarterly and annually (eg profit margins, cost recoveries and so on)

* senior managers (organization-wide and IT directorate) are satisfied with the reports produced

* the cost management system is delivering the expected benefits (see 6.1)

* faults are fixed according to Problem Management and Change Management targets and guidelines

* cost recovery plans are on target (cost recovery provides a barometer of how well prices have been set in relation to predicted costings of IT usage).

The IT Services Manager is responsible for this first post-implementation review and also for ensuring that an annual audit of the cost management system is carried out using the same broad guidelines. The Cost Manager performs this type of audit on a quarterly basis initially and six-monthly after the project has been in successful operation for one year. Where possible, attempt to synchronize reviews with those which take place for Service Level Agreements(SLAs).

5.1.2 Ongoing operation

The day-to-day operation of the cost management system covers many of the functions discussed in section 5.1.1, since the activities of the cost management system cover collection of data, monitoring, reviewing, projecting costs and setting charges. A brief checklist of the ongoing activities is given below:

Daily/Weekly

* ongoing collection of cost data and charging data

* instigate changes, if necessary (see also 5.1.3)

* attend Change Advisory Boards (CAB) as required.

Monthly

* as above

* run the cost management reporting system

* recalculate business unit and standard unit costs to check for conformance with predicted results

* produce invoices

* collect income

* review the cost management system to ensure that the IT Directorate business objectives are being met

* circulate a monthly balance sheet (see Annex E)

* monitor cost recovery plots

* analyze any variances.

Quarterly

* as for daily/weekly/monthly items, plus a full-scale audit of the system for conformance with expectation

* assess from collected data the accuracy of the charging algorithms by balancing the actual revenue against expected revenue (similarly for actual costs against predicted)

* assess the accuracy of forecasts as a means of improving them in the future

* verify the price lists

* using current data, plan the changes necessary for next year's cost management staff and resources, and any alterations to cost projections and cost recovery projections.

Annually

* all of the foregoing tasks must also be carried out on an annual basis, audit the system under the responsibility of the organization's computer audit section which is independent of the IT Services section (see 5.1.7)

* re-publish reviewed price lists, cost projections, cost recovery projections, standard and business unit costs.

5.1.3 Change management

The cost management system, when running in production, is based on an annual cycle for which plans and budgets are produced. Costs incurred and revenue earned are then compared against these plans and budgets. If fundamental changes to the system are needed they should be aligned to this annual cycle. If changes cannot wait to be implemented until the beginning of a new financial year, there may be severe consequences involving users (prices may have to go up, costs must be curtailed, demand reduced and so on). It may be possible to arrange for packages of changes to be aligned to the changes made to SLAs.

Where changes are unavoidable, their introduction must be subject to change management procedures. Small-scale changes must also be subject to change management. Such small-scale changes can, however, be made through short-term special arrangements, but must be included in the cost management system for the coming financial year.

Agree all decisions about changes to the system under the auspices of change management, with representatives from:

* service level management

* cost management

* IT Services management.

If customers are affected, user management must also participate in the decision making.

Example reasons for change

With a complex cost management system there may be many reasons for changes needing to be made. Examples of these are:

* errors in the cost management or associated systems leading to incorrect forecasts, budgets or calculations

* workloads greater or less than forecast.

Workloads greater or less than forecast would lead to resource usage different from predicted usage, in turn leading to:

* recovery of greater or less than predicted amounts

* variance in workload or resources

* customers exceed their budgets.

Errors and variance

Careful monitoring of the system during the recommended pilot phase reduces the likelihood that major changes will become necessary and where changes are identified, certainly lessens their impact.

Errors must be rectified at source to prevent recurrence; where forecasts are at variance with actuals, the appropriate cost plans, cost recovery plans, and in some instances, charges, must be altered. Identify such variance in forecasts and use the experience to prevent recurrence.

It is recommended that where charging is introduced (real or notional) the charges should **not** be altered - even during the pilot - unless serious errors are discovered which have caused very large variance in recovery forecasts leading to severe over-charging (and of course, excessive revenue) or under-charging leading to severe losses.

Where price lists **must** be altered and charges raised or lowered, give advance notice to provide a warning to users about the impact of the impending changes on their budgets.

Customer budget problems Explicit in the organization SLA should be statements about what happens should a customer exceed the allotted budget. The statements should cover this eventuality where:

* there is no spare resource

* spare capacity is available.

In any organization it is likely that the importance of the business in question will directly affect the contingency plan for this sort of problem. In every case however, the first question to answer is who foots the bill - the second is how!

In Government it is likely that spare capacity, if available, would be provided and the IT Services section asked to account for the increased costs. If spare capacity were not available, it might be necessary to engage a bureau or even to upgrade machine capacity. The cost would probably be met centrally, but it is very important to ensure that SLAs are not compromised and are specific on these issues.

The organization may need to consider whether a customer is allowed to continue to use resources to the detriment of other customers - but not IT Services - if the business is particularly important. Every case, however, is likely to require a management decision and mechanisms must be in place to cater for such problems.

Unit cost variance Standard unit costs (see Annex D) are planned costs of the components of IT services. The Cost Manager calculates the cost of a measurable unit of CPU (it could be decided that CPU seconds is the unit of measure) for various types of service (on-line, batch, system software). The standard unit cost is compared to the actual costs. This standard unit cost comparison is then a barometer of the accuracy of the planning data.

The standard unit cost comparison is also a barometer of service quality; if the actual unit costs are considerably less than the planned standard unit costs, the initial reaction may well be one of euphoria. Temper this euphoria until it is identified whether or not the cheaper unit costs are the result of poorer service quality!

Where forecasts are inaccurate, lower-than-planned unit costs may indicate either cost savings by IT Services or greater-than-planned use of resources by the users. If it is the latter, it does not matter if there is spare capacity. If capacity is at a premium it is likely that service quality has suffered. Action must be taken to curb the unplanned demand until it can be accommodated, or to establish the business relevance of the demand. Such action is the responsibility of the Capacity Manager.

When spare capacity is plentiful, its ad hoc use must not set a precedent. Spare capacity is usually earmarked for future use (indeed it is profligate to maintain plentiful spare capacity). Customers wishing to increase their use of resources on a long-term basis must provide a business case and obtain authorization via the normal channels. It is vital that the SLAs made with other customers are adhered to and not compromised to accommodate a single customer.

Revenue variance

Although the organization may decide to run the IT services at a profit, it is possible that monitoring reveals either too great a profit (leading to user dissatisfaction) or a shortfall. Where too much revenue is generated the cause must be identified and justified or corrected; unless absolutely necessary the charges must not be altered. Some of the reasons for generating excessive revenue include:

* bad service - customers are forced to buy more IT resource because the workload cannot be handled by the capacity and overtime is being worked and paid for

* workload growth is faster than forecast with similar consequences

* charges really are excessive.

Where a poor service is the difficulty, the underlying causes must be addressed. When workload growth is a problem, forecasts must be revised (otherwise trouble is being stored) and it may become necessary to make a case to procure additional capacity.

If the IT services are sustaining a loss, possible causes include:

* running insufficient work (perhaps forecasts of workload were too high)

* running costs are too high (perhaps because of too much overtime or staffing is above complement)

* charges really are too low.

Once more, forecast revision may become necessary. Where running costs are the problem, the IT Services section may have to examine the possibility of making economies.

5.1.4 Ongoing planning

If there is a long lead-time between the tactical planning and the bring-into-service date of the plan (ie the start of the financial year to which it applies) it may become necessary to revise the cost plans, projections and so on. Cost planning should begin at least three months prior to the start of the financial year, because of the complexity of the planning processes. Remember that the data used in the plan will require revision after publication, because it will be out of date.

Any changes to IT capacity (or indeed any other IT or human resources) that were not present in the tactical plans must be reported to the Cost Manager for inclusion in revised cost plans, projections and so on.

Typically, workload changes as agreed at SLA reviews must also be reported. Cost implications and charging implications must be explicit in SLAs. SLA changes are normally aligned to tactical plan production, but IT Services management may delegate to the Service Level Manager powers to vary SLAs within agreed bounds during the tactical planning process (typically at the mid-year point, see the IT Infrastructure Library **Service Level Management** module). See also 5.1.3.

5.1.5 Contingency planning

Section 4.3 discusses contingency options which may become necessary, stressing the need to keep manual records where the cost management system has to be withdrawn. The Cost Manager should also discover which reports and plans are indispensable to the organization and ensure that they are produced manually in the event of a disaster affecting the cost management system. These needs should be kept under regular review. The impact of a disaster is minimized by keeping off-site back-up of all required data and by maintaining standby or spare equipment upon which to run the cost management system. See also the IT Infrastructure Library **Contingency Planning** module.

5.1.6 Management reporting

Regular monthly reports for each supported business are required. Prepare a monthly summary of costs and revenue for the IT Services Manager, together with a balance sheet. Senior IT management committees may also require a report, probably each quarter.

Although the format of management reports is largely dependent on the standards set by the organization it is suggested that reports to business customers include details about how:

* much they have spent on IT during the financial year

* the changes made match the predicted profile

* the costs and charges are itemized

* the revenue is being used to improve IT.

Reports to the IT Services Manager should cover:

* total IT costs

* costs broken down by each business supported

* total revenue

* revenue broken down by each business

* costs and cost recovery against profile

* outlook on costs and cost recovery

* any problems

* any recommendations for changes

* future investments

* cost of waste.

Senior IT executive committee (ITEC) reports should contain similar information. Reports produced by efficiency and effectiveness reviews of the cost management system and audit reports are also of interest to the ITEC (as mentioned in 5.1.1 and 5.1.7) and these should include details of any recommendations that were followed up from previous reports.

Annex E contains some suggested formats for the more technical reports such as balance sheets and profit and loss statements.

5.1.7 Auditing the processes

Procedural audits may be performed internally or by external auditors. In both instances audits are intended to confirm that the Cost Manager and the supporting personnel are adhering to defined procedures. Management should however operate its own controls and not rely on audit, whether internal or external. The Cost Manager will therefore perform his own audits and checks to reassure management that the system runs properly and is policed effectively. Independent audit will confirm this reassurance and also comment on efficiency and suggest improvements that may be identified. Examples of items to be audited include:

* reviews are carried out regularly and followed up

* regular and accurate reports are produced for management (also includes the production of price lists)

* the appropriate configuration management items (CIs) are up-to-date and accurate

* change and problem management procedures are adhered to

* service level management targets are met.

The computer audit team should also:

* randomly select invoices to test for accuracy

* examine cost recovery projections and revenue to assess the accuracy of the system

* ensure that audit trails are provided

* ensure that revenues are collected and properly accounted for

* check that all documentation is accurate, up to-date and complete.

5.2   Dependencies

The dependencies listed at 3.2 and 4.2 also apply to the post-implementation processes.

5.3   People

The Cost Manager has responsibility for the overall running of the cost management system.

The Director of IT should arrange for regular efficiency and effectiveness reviews of the cost management function to be carried out by:

* the Cost Manager

* the IT Services Manager

* independent computer audit teams (annually).

It is likely that the Cost Manager needs support to carry out the work. In a small organization (one or two small mainframes) the functions of cost and capacity management could probably be combined so long as a team of about four individuals is available to support both capacity and cost management functions.

In larger organizations a full-time Cost Manager will require up to four staff: large organizations need to assess staff requirements depending on the volumes of data, numbers of business users and whether the organization is distributed across different locations.

5.4   Timing

Timing of the reviews and audits is described in 5.1.2, together with frequency of management reporting.

6. Benefits, costs and possible problems

6.1 Benefits

As costing and charging are two separate but related activities, they service two diverse purposes, and thereby provide different benefits.

6.1.1 Costing

The fundamental benefit of costing IT services is that it provides management information on the costs of providing IT services that support the organization's business needs. This information is needed to enable IT management to make decisions that ensure the IT Services section runs in a cost effective manner. Cost effectiveness is defined here as ensuring that there is a proper balance between the quality of service on the one side and expenditure on the other. Any investment that increases the costs of providing IT services must always result in enhancement to service quality or quantity: this also applies to the introduction of cost management.

Costing helps the IT Services Manager to:

* base decisions about the services to be provided on assessments of cost-effectiveness, service by service

* make more business-like decisions about IT services and investments in them

* provide information to justify IT expenditures

* plan and budget with confidence

* understand the costs of failing to take advantage of strategic opportunities to justify the required expenditure (thereby providing value-added productivity).

Put simply, there is no prospect of IT service providers maximizing value for money if the costs of providing the services are not accurately known. Costing is therefore essential.

6.1.2 Strategic opportunities

New or better business opportunity through the use of IT is a key justification for investing in more resources. Cost management identifies the likely costs of supporting these opportunities.

Strategic opportunities are concerned with positioning the
IT Services section in preparation for future workload
demands and can be grouped as follows:

* opportunities to provide new services:

    - to prepare for workload types that could not have
      been performed without IT

    - to address the requirements of customers that
      have so far not benefited from the services of the
      IT Services section

* opportunities to provide better services:

    - targeting, to prepare for workloads that enable
      the IT Services section to be more precise in
      servicing the right customers in the best way

    - more effective management, to prepare for
      workloads that enable the IT Services section to
      make use of resources to ensure a quality service
      for its clients.

6.1.3 Value-added productivity

Value-added productivity is concerned with IT services
being part of the business process and thereby enhancing
the quality of the end-product emerging from that process.

There are three types of benefits:

* quality-added processes, which provide services to
  carry out business processes in such a way that they
  provide better quality

* time-saving features, which provide services that
  carry out the business process more quickly or with
  fewer human resources, thereby showing improved
  efficiency

* value-added charging, which provides services that
  enable the business process to deliver additional
  products that could not have been delivered without
  IT.

6.1.4   Charging

The fundamental benefit of charging customers is that it provides a business interface between the IT Services section and its customers. Customers are charged for the services they receive and because they are paying, they have a right to expect a good service. If they do not think the charges represent value for money, they can stop using the services or complain to the organization's management. If IT Services management think they can improve services by spending more on IT, they can do so (providing they justify the expenditure). If customers believe that they save money by changing the way in which they use the IT services, they will do so.

Charging enables the IT Services management to:

* allow business-like evaluations of IT services and plan for investment based on cost recovery and business benefits

* recover IT costs in a fair manner, related to system usage

* influence customer behaviour (eg, by charging more at peak times, encouraging off-peak usage).

Unlike costing, the introduction of hard charging (ie actual money changing hands) is not absolutely essential. The cost of introducing hard charging should be outweighed by better value for money for customers and providers: the nature of IT systems often militates against this. System constraints may mean that it is not possible to provide a higher (or lower) quality of service to an individual customer even if that customer is prepared to pay (or sacrifice) for it.

Hard charging is therefore desirable in principle but introduction must actually influence behaviour to improve value for money and do so to an extent that savings outweigh administrative costs.

Notional charging is, essentially, introduced to ensure that customers are aware of the costs they incur. The effectiveness of introducing notional charging depends on the supporting management processes: if customers ignore the information and management takes no action, there is little point in providing the information.

Charging, whether hard or notional should be introduced only when the organization is convinced of the benefits to be gained.

6.2   Costs

The costs associated with cost management fall into two broad categories:

* the administration and organization costs for the planning, implementation and ongoing operations and management of the function (ie people)

* tools required to carry out the processes (some of these tools are also required for other IT Infrastructure Library functions).

6.3   Possible problems

There are a number of possible problems:

* costing (**not** charging) is very often a new discipline in IT Services, and little information is currently available to guide organizations

* costing relies on planning information provided by other functions both within and outside of IT Services management, which might not yet be available

* staff combining accountancy and IT experience are rare

* organizations' IS strategies and objectives may not be well formulated and documented (thus direction is lacking)

* failure to recognize the potential of such a system

* lack of management commitment.

Where cost management is not practised, it is common to discover that the organization is not able to respond to demand for their IT services in a business-like and proactive manner.

Care should be taken to ensure that the costing and charging processes are not so elaborate that the cost of the system exceeds the value of the information produced!

The problems identified in this sub-section may be alleviated if the organization implements the guidance contained in this module.

7. Tools

Tools required for cost management are often shared, or at least made available, by various other people within IT infrastructure management (for example the Capacity Manager and the Configuration Manager). Although tools covered in this section are described from a cost management point of view, their use is not necessarily specific and exclusive to cost management.

Where tools described perform a function in the area of say, capacity management, more information can be found in the appropriate IT Infrastructure Library module.

Proprietary products mentioned in this section are examples of tools which, at the time of writing, are available for use and function as described.

7.1 Types of tools

The tools needed for cost management can be categorized into five types, as shown below:

* data recording

* database (configuration management)

* reports

* plans

* special applications.

Each type is described in more detail in the following sections.

The choice of each type of tool depends on whether it is to be mainframe (m/f) or Personal Computer (PC) based. For mainframe tools the choice depends on the workloads involved and the hardware architecture.

7.1.1 Data recording

Data recording tools are concerned with providing data on workload usage, service levels and costs. The data about workload and service levels is normally obtained from system monitoring software, collected and maintained by capacity management and service level management. Cost information is captured using the organization's accounting practices.

Workload usage	There are three basic types of tools for collecting workload information:

> * general, workload oriented (for example IBM SMF and ICL SYSTEM MONITOR)
>
> * general, system-wide (for example IBM RMF and ICL VCMS)
>
> * workload-specific (for example IBM CMF and ULTRACOMP SCEPTRE.)

These tools are all mainframe-based.

Service levels	Service level information is provided from the applications themselves. Most applications are written so that for example, business unit counts are routinely made and to a limited extent this is true of some workload related tools. Often product management databases also contain relevant information (m/f).
Performance database	The performance database consolidates and summarizes workload and service information and is used by capacity management to produce tabular and graphical reports on workload and system usage. In the costing and charging context, a performance database serves the purpose of a consolidated information base for workload and service information (m/f).
Costs	Cost data will come from accounting and information systems and any relevant additional feeder system. The data will normally be collated and summarized in spreadsheet format on a PC.
Manpower	IT Services manpower represents one of the largest costs involved in providing IT services. A system for recording time spent on specific service provision activities is needed.

7.1.2 Databases

Database tools are used to hold and maintain selected and prepared data for forecasting and rate calculations, and form the basis of the management reporting tools. They can be either mainframe or PC based dependent on the size and complexity of the system. For cost management purposes alone, they are normally PC based.

Resources	Resource inventories hold inventory and cost information on computer hardware, communications, software, facilities and the organization. The prime objective is to provide information that easily fits the rate calculations. (PC). (If a configuration management database is available, it may hold the required data).

Deliverables	Service and workload inventories provide the interface between the performance database and the requirements of costing. The prime objective is to provide information that easily fits in with the rate calculations. (PC)
Finances	Cost and income inventories hold information about actual expenditures and real income; they form the interface to the organization's accounts payable and accounts receivable. (PC)

7.1.3 Reporting

Reporting tools are concerned with the manipulation and summary of the data in the various databases. The tools can be either mainframe or PC based dependent on the size and complexity of the costing requirements and the location of the databases to be maintained.

7.1.4 Planning

Planning tools can be used to perform the rate calculations and provide all the required business analysis and reports. The inputs are the workload and service projections from capacity planning and service level management. These are normally maintained for cost management in the various databases mentioned above. (PC)

7.1.5 Special applications

Tools for special applications are needed to interface the cost management system to the outside world. A typical example is the billing system that issues invoices to customers.

General Ledger Package (GLP)	GLPs allow comparison of costs and budgets and provide a comprehensive set of IT Cost Centre analyses. It must be realized that GLPs differ and that some can be tailored to suit the needs of the organization.
Accounting packages	Accounting packages carry a slightly misleading name, as they are mostly concerned with charging and billing. They are specialized versions of performance databases that translate workload and service usage information into monetary terms, based on a preselected rate/price structure. (m/f)
	An example is GAP (Government Accounting Package) for ICL and IBM mainframes.

7.2 Package selection

To select a cost management package of any of the types described in 7.1, the following actions should be carried out:

* formalize the requirements definition; confirm the functionality and present it in a format that aids the selection process

* develop an evaluation method; determine the relative importance of each requirement and produce a requirements matrix with an assigned weighting for each factor

* invite responses from suppliers; from the requirement definition provide a statement for potential package suppliers, and issue to about three suppliers. Choose potential vendors who are known to have successful operational packages; for Government departments, preferably with a reference site in the public sector

* evaluate bidders' proposals; for at least two bidders evaluate the response, including telephoning reference sites and attending a demonstration by the bidder, and review the bidders' documentation

* choose and implement a package.

This is a brief summary of guidance which is provided in the CCTA Application and Evaluation Library.

7.3 Interface requirements

Tools used in cost management must be able to interface with data collected and maintained by capacity management, service level management and configuration management.

7.4 Current tools

The current market place for specialized cost management tools concentrates on accounting packages. In the industry there are a large number of bespoke applications developed by individual data centres to fulfil their own needs for cost management. These applications are most often large mainframe application suites. PC spreadsheets are mostly used by accounts departments, for consolidation and reconciliation.

7.5 Advantages and pitfalls

The advantages of using cost management software tools are that they provide quicker results by saving, like all tools, time and effort. The disadvantages are of two kinds, depending on the type of tool. Firstly, for accounting packages, they may not fit the structure that the IT Services section wants for its cost management system, and therefore may have to undergo substantial customization.

Secondly, for spreadsheets, they are merely packages in which an application has to be developed, and thereby require substantial accounting skills, as well skills in the use of spreadsheets, to produce a competent result.

7.6 Future

The requirements of cost management tools will most probably include:

* integrated PC applications to perform the planning and management reporting

* interfaces to existing accounting packages which can provide more sophisticated billing algorithms

* standards in applications development to log business unit details as they are being processed.

7.7 Shortcomings

There are currently no tools on the market that monitor and record business units, and it is unlikely, even in the longer term, that such monitoring will be possible unless individual programs/applications are designed to provide the information.

8.　Bibliography

Accounting for Data Processing Costs
McGee, Robert W; 87/05, Auerbach Publishers,
Winter 1987, Journal of Accounting and EDP

Accounting for Information Centre Cost
Hoshower, Leon B and Verstraete, Anthony A;
86/05, Auerbach Publishers, Winter 1986 Journal of
Accounting and EDP

Appraisal and Evaluation Library
CCTA

Chargeout of Information Systems Services
Choudhury, Nanadan; Sircar, Sumit and Venkata, K;
86/09 - September 1986 Journal of Systems
Management

Computer Capacity: A Production Control Approach
Strauss, Melvin J, 1981 - van Nostrand Reinhold
Company

Computer Effectiveness: Bridging the Management
Technology Gap
Axelrod, C Warren; 1979, Information Resources
Press

Computer Productivity: A Planning Guide for Cost
Effective Management
1982, John Wiley & Sons

Data Processing Budgets: How to develop and use Budgets
Effectively (A Management Perspective)
1985 - Prentice - Hall, Inc

Data Processor's Survival Guide to Accounting
Perry, William E; 1985 - John Wiley & Sons Inc

Establishing an IS Management System
Morino, Mario; 86/09 - 1986 Morino Associates

Evaluating the returns from information technology
Lincoln, Dr Tim; 86/04 - April 1986 Management
Accounting

Financial Management of Computing
Chartered Institute of Public Finance and
Accountancy (CIPFA), 1982

Information Services as Profit Centre
> Kull, David; 85/12, Hayden Publishing Co.,
> December 1985, Computer Decisions

Installation Accounting with MICS
> Morino Associates; 85/ - 1985 MICS Evaluation
> Series

Management Accounting
Official Technology
> Chartered Institute of Management Accountants
> (CIMA), 1989

Mapping Chargeback Systems to Organizations
Environments
> McKinnon, William P and Kallman, Ernest A;
> 87/03 - March 1987 MIS Quarterly

MIS Budget Dilemma
> Ewing, Tom; 87/04 - April 20 1987 Information
> WEEK

Planning, Budgeting and Control for Data Processing
> Francl, T; Lin, T and Vasarhelyi, M; 1984 - Van
> Nostrand Reinhold Books

The Success of IT Chargeback Systems from a User's
Perception
> Bergeron, Francois; 86/04 - April 1986 Information &
> Management

When is Chargeback Counterproductive
> Stevens, David F; 86/07, Applied Computer
> Research, July 1986, EDP Performance Review

Fees and charges: A guide for Government Departments
{1983 (revised edition) - currently under further revision}

Improving Management in Government: the Next Steps

Economic Appraisal in Central Government: A Technical
Guide for Government Departments

Investment Appraisal in the Public Sector: A Technical
Guide for Government Departments

Government Accounting: A Guide on Accounting and
Financial Procedures for the use of Government
Departments

Trading Accounts: A Guide for Government Departments
and Non-Departmental Public Bodies
> HM Treasury

Annex A. Glossary of terms

Acronyms and abbreviations used in this module

ACC	Accommodation Cost Centre
ACU	Accommodation Cost Unit
CMDB	Configuration Management Database
CPU	Central Processing Unit
CRAMM	CCTA Risk Analysis and Management Method
CSBC	Computer Services Business Centre
DGL	Departmental General Ledger
ECC	Equipment Cost Centre
ECU	Equipment Cost Unit
I/O	Input/Output
IS	Information Services or Systems
IT	Information Technology
IWR	Indirect Workload Rate
MB	Megabyte
M/F	Mainframe
MIPS	Millions of Instructions Per Second
OCC	Organization Cost Centre
OCU	Organizational Cost Unit
OIE	Organization Indirect Equipment
OIW	Organization Indirect Workload
PC	Personal Computer
PRINCE	PRojects IN Controlled Environments
RFC	Request For Change
SCC	Software Cost Centre
SCU	Software Cost Unit
SIW	Software Indirect Workload

SLA	Service Level Agreement
SLM	Service Level Management
SSADM	Structured Systems Analysis and Design Methodology
TOR	Terms of Reference
TCC	Transfer Cost Centre
TCU	Transfer Cost Unit
WCC	Workload Cost Centre

Definitions used in this module

Absorbed overhead	Overhead which, by means of absorption rates, is included in costs of specific products or saleable services, in a given period of time.
	Under or over-absorbed overhead. The difference between overhead cost incurred and overhead cost absorbed: it may be split into its two constituent parts for control purposes.
Absorption costing	A principle whereby fixed as well as variable costs are allotted to cost units and total overheads are absorbed according to activity level.
	The term may be applied where production costs only, or costs of all functions are so allotted.
Allocated cost	A cost that can be directly identified with a business unit.
Apportioned cost	A cost that is shared by a number of business units (an indirect cost). This cost must be shared out between these units on an equitable basis.
Business unit	A segment of the business entity by which both revenues are received and expenditure are caused or controlled, such revenues and expenditure being used to evaluate segmental performance.
Capital investment appraisal	The process of evaluating proposed investment in specific fixed assets and the benefits to be obtained from their acquisition.
	The techniques used in the evaluation can be summarized as non-discounting methods (ie simple pay-back), return on capital employed and discounted cash flow methods (ie yield, net present value and discounted pay-back).
Charging	The process of establishing charges in respect of business units, and raising the relevant invoices for recovery from customers.

Cost	The amount of expenditure (actual or notional) incurred on, or attributable to, a specific activity or business unit.
Costing	The process of identifying the costs of the business and of breaking them down and relating them to the various activities of the organization.
Cost management	The term used in this module to describe all the procedures, tasks and deliverables that are needed to fulfil an organization's costing and charging requirements.
Cost unit	In the context of CSBC the cost unit is a functional cost unit which establishes standard cost per workload element of activity, based on calculated activity ratios converted to cost ratios.
Depreciation	Depreciation is the loss in value of an asset due to its use and/or the passage of time. The annual depreciation charge in accounts represents the amount of capital assets used up in the accounting period. It is charged in the cost accounts to ensure that the cost of capital equipment is reflected in the unit costs of the services provided using the equipment. There are various methods of calculating depreciation for the period, but the Treasury usually recommend the use of current cost asset valuation as the basis for the depreciation charge. See Annex D.4.
Differential charging	Charging business customers different rates for the same work, typically to dampen demand or to generate revenue for spare capacity. This can also be used to encourage off-peak or night time running.
Direct cost	A cost which is incurred for, and can be traced in full to a product, service, cost centre or department. This is an **allocated** cost. Direct costs are direct materials, direct wages and direct expenses.
Discounted cash flow	An evaluation of the future net cash flows generated by a capital project, by discounting them to their present-day value.

The two methods most commonly used are:

a yield method, for which the calculation determines the internal rate of return (IRR) in the form of a percentage,

b net present value (NPV) method, in which the discount rate is chosen and the answer is a sum of money.

Discounting	Discounting is the offering to business customers of reduced rates for the use of off-peak resources (see also Surcharging).
Elements of cost	The constituent parts of costs according to the factors upon which expenditure is incurred viz, materials, labour and expenses.
Financial year	The financial year is an accounting period covering 12 consecutive months. In the public sector this financial year will generally coincide with the fiscal year which runs from 1 April to 31 March.
Full cost	Full cost is the total cost of all the resources used in supplying a service ie the sum of the direct costs of producing the output, a proportional share of overhead costs and any selling and distribution expenses. Both cash costs and notional (non-cash) costs should be included, including the cost of capital.
Indirect cost	An indirect cost is a cost incurred in the course of making a product, providing a service or running a cost centre or department, but which cannot be traced directly and in full to the product, service or department, because it has been incurred for a number of cost centres or cost units. These costs are **apportioned** to cost centres/cost units. Indirect costs are also referred to as **overheads**.
Marginal cost	The variable cost of producing one extra unit of product or service. That is, the cost which would have been avoided if the unit/service was not produced/provided.
Opportunity cost (or true cost)	The value of a benefit sacrificed in favour of an alternative course of action. That is the cost of using resources in a particular operation expressed in terms of foregoing the benefit that could be derived from the best alternative use of those resources.
Overheads	The total of indirect materials, wages and expenses.
Prime cost	The total cost of direct materials, direct labour and direct expenses. The term prime cost is commonly restricted to direct production costs only and so does not customarily include direct costs of marketing or research and development.

Resource unit costs	Resource unit may be calculated on a standard cost basis to identify the expected (standard) cost for using a particular resource. Because computer resources come in many shapes and forms, units have to be established by logical groupings. Examples are:
	
	  * CPU time or instructions
	
	  * disk I/Os
	
	  * print lines
	
	  * communication transactions.

Resources	The term resources refers to the means the IT Services section needs to provide the customers with the required services. The resources are typically computer and related equipment, software, facilities or organizational (people).
Services	Services are the deliverables of the IT Services section as perceived by the customers; the services do not consist merely of making computer resources available for customers to use.
Software work unit	Software work is a generic term devised to represent a common base on which all calculations for workload usage and IT resource capacity are then based. A unit of software work for I/O type equipment equals the number of **bytes transferred**; and for central processors it is based on the product of **power** and **cpu-time**.
Standard cost	A pre-determined calculation of how much costs should be under specified working conditions. It is built up from an assessment of the value of cost elements and correlates technical specifications and the quantification of materials, labour and other costs to the prices and/or wages expected to apply during the period in which the standard cost is intended to be used. Its main purposes are to provide bases for control through variance accounting, for the valuation of work in progress and for fixing selling prices.
Standard costing	A technique which uses standards for costs and revenues for the purposes of control through variance analysis.
Storage occupancy	Storage occupancy is a defined measurement unit that is used for storage type equipment to measure usage: the unit value equals the number of bytes stored.
Surcharging	Surcharging is charging business users a premium rate for using resources at peak times.

Unit costs	Unit costs are costs distributed over individual component usage to establish the unit cost. For example, it can be assumed, that if a box of paper with 1,000 sheets costs £10, then obviously one sheet costs 1p. Similarly if a CPU costs £1m a year and it is used to process 1,000 jobs that year, each job costs on average £1,000.
Utility cost centre (UCC)	A cost centre for the provision of support services to other cost centres.
Variance analysis	A variance is the difference between planned, budgeted, or standard cost and actual cost (or revenues). Variance analysis is an analysis of the factors which have caused the difference between the pre-determined standards and the actual results. Variances can be developed specifically related to the operations carried out in addition to those mentioned above.

Annex B. Sample Terms of Reference

Terms of Reference establish the scope of cost management from the viewpoints of:

* benefits

* what?

* why?

* how?

* who?

* when?

* input requirements

* output requirements

* cost

* risks

* constraints.

The contents of the Terms of Reference outlined below are an **example**. Tailor the contents to suit the needs of your organization.

B.1 Purpose

The purpose of this project is to provide a cost effective cost management system with the correct scope and deliverables for this IT Services section.

B.2 Aim

The aim is to ensure that all the requirements concerning the organization's business and management practices are evaluated and understood so that the implemented system reflects the way the IT Services section is to do business and to provide the necessary information for decision making and charging.

B.3 Stages

The stages of this project can briefly be described as:

* Stage 1 - Feasibility study

    - to establish the feasible solutions for cost management (this stage is not always required)

    * Stage 2 - Development (which includes systems analysis and design)

       - to establish and document detailed business and management requirements

       - to design the selected solution

    * Stage 3 - Testing

       - to validate the proposals

       - to verify that the developed system meets functional and business needs

    * Stage 4 - Implementation

       - to implement the developed system

    * Stage 5 - Post-implementation

       - to integrate the implemented system into the existing management activities.

Systems analysis and design should conform to SSADM guidelines. The project should be controlled using PRINCE guidance.

B.4 Responsibilities

The responsibility for this project lies at different stages with:

* the project manager
* a qualified accountant
* the future business/cost manager
* a technical expert from systems programming.

B.5 Timescales

Detail the development time and testing deadlines.

For example: if the development time is scheduled to take 7 months with all testing to be completed by 1 November; data recording can cover the six months period ending 31 October. Parallel running with existing system is planned to run from 1 December through to 28 February, and cut over at 1 April, the start of the financial year.

The feasibility study report can outline an implementation plan for the proposed cost management system.

B.6 Requirements

The information requirements of this project include:

* capacity management: usage data from the performance database and planning data from workload forecasting

* cost data from the financial/ management accounting and information systems

* service level management: business component data

* IT Services management: strategies, policies and operation.

B.7 Deliverables

The deliverable from this project is a system for cost management that supports:

* planning and budget setting on an annual basis

* production of management reports on a monthly basis

* generation of invoices on a monthly basis.

B.8 Staff resources and tools

An example of staff resources and tools that may be required are:

* 1 full time project manager for 12 months

* 1 full time Cost Manager

* IT Services Manager (10% of his time over approximately 12 months elapsed time)

* SSADM expert (half time over approximately 12 months elapsed time)

* 1 half-time senior systems programmer for 12 months

* a qualified accountant or where unavailable Internal Audit Consultancy (50 man days)

* Internal Audit Consultancy (50 man days)

* 1 PC

* 1 PC/mainframe interface

* 1 PC spreadsheet package

* 1 PC database management system

* 1 PC word processor

* 1 mainframe invoicing system

* various measurement tools and performance databases, dependent on what is currently used.

B.9 Job description for Cost Manager

Main duties

1 Specifies, initiates and maintains the cost management system and information structure including cost centres, classifications of workload and equipment requirements and so on as described in this module.

2 Supervises the collation of all costs associated with the provision of IT services.

3 Responsible for the production of cost recovery plans and charging algorithms (where appropriate).

4 Supervises the monitoring of IT service costs to ensure that business objectives (including the creation of profits from IT service provision, where appropriate) are achieved.

5 Publicizes the cost management system to the organization, ensures that all users are familiar with procedures and are satisfied with the day-to-day operation of the system.

6 Analyzes and reviews the cost management system on a regular basis to ensure its effectiveness and to recommend improvements where needed.

7 Attends Change Advisory Board (CAB) meetings.

8 Produces regular reports about the effectiveness of the system for the IT Directorate.

9 Responsible for preparing the cost management sections of IT strategic and tactical plans.

B.10 Budget

The feasibility study report outlines the cost of the project (based on the staffing required, accommodation costs and related expenditure as indicated in B.8). A budget for the cost management system can then be set which is controlled by the Project Board.

Annex C. Feasibility study

C.1 Feasibility study

The feasibility study has the objective of establishing feasible solutions to the requirements outlined in the Terms of Reference (see Annex B).

C.2 Identify and document current situation

The first task is a detailed analysis to establish the extent to which cost management is currently being carried out. The analysis:

* identifies current practices

* establishes current responsibilities

* identifies tools used

* establishes information flow.

The two matrices (figures C1 and C2) are used to help carry out this task.

The responsibilities matrix (figure C1) is used to establish the functions currently being performed and the extent to which they are achieving objectives.

The responsibilities matrix is filled in by answering the following questions:

* who is responsible for each function? - if one or more people are identified, put an "R" in the cell(s) that corresponds to both the function and the person(s)

* who needs to approve the deliverables from the function? - if anybody not on part of the standard management hierarchy is identified, put an "A" in the cell(s) that corresponds to both the function and the person(s)

* who is working in or with the function? - if one or more people are identified, put an "S" in the cell(s) that corresponds to both the function and the person(s)

* does anybody need to be kept informed about the progress of the work of the function? - if one or more is identified, put an "I" in the cell(s) that corresponds to both the function and the person

* to what extent is the function operating according to IT Infrastructure Library principles and practices, or equivalent? - indicate the current capabilities of the function on a scale from 1 to 5, where 1 is just getting started and 5 is fully operational.

After filling in the matrix analyze the result by looking at the distribution of responsibilities:

* are there many people involved or is the work done by one or two people

* are there active functions with no one responsible or are there active functions with more than one person responsible?

* are there functions with little or no manpower (all Chiefs and no Indians)?

* are there functions where authority does not follow responsibility?

* is there an even level of capabilities across functions?

The responsibilities matrix analyzes the health of IT infrastructure management such as service level management and workload management that are particularly relevant to cost management. Guidance on the operation of these functions is contained in other IT Infrastructure Library modules, including, in particular:

* Capacity Management

* Change Management

* Computer Operations Management

* Configuration Management

* Contingency Planning

* Management of Local Processors and Terminals

* Network Management

* Planning and Control

* Problem Management

* Service Level Management.

ITIL Responsibilities Matrix	Organization							Level (1-5)
IT Management Application development projects IT services management.								

SERVICE LEVEL MANAGEMENT.
Include business unit analysis
      Service inventories
      Service catalogue
      Service level establishment
      Service level agreements								

CHANGE MANAGEMENT.
Include RFC logging
      Impact analysis
      Change authors
      Change schedules
      Change building
      Change testing
      Change review								

PROBLEM MANAGEMENT.
Include problem logging/allocation
      problem tracking
      problem fixing								

WORKLOAD MANAGEMENT.
Include Workload inventories
      Workload characterization
      Workload forecasting
      Mainframe planning								

IT RESOURCE MANAGEMENT.
Include Network planning
      Planning for end user
      computing/office automation
      Contingency/Recovery planning
      Physical planning								

CONFIGURATION MANAGEMENT. Include Hardware/Software inventories								

COST MANAGEMENT.
Include Standard unit costing
      Business unit costing
      Charging
      Cost accounting
      Facilities inventory (Accommodation)								

FORMAL PLANNING Include IS Strategic plans IT Tactical plans								

SYSTEM MONITORING
Include Information bases
      Performance database
      Instrumentation								

Figure C1: Responsibilities matrix

C.3 The measurement tools matrix

The matrix (figure C2) is used to identify the tools currently in use and the type of information they provide.

The matrix is completed by identifying the tools providing information on resource usage and service levels by individual workload types - for example, identifying which tools measure CPU-time, which tools measure disk storage and disk I/Os and so on.

After filling in the matrix, analyze the result by identifying any areas not being measured; pay particular attention if this applies particularly to specific workloads and/or types of equipment.

In addition to the matrix analysis it is also necessary to identify the types of tools available. Classify them according to the structure outlined in section 7.

Measurement tools analysis Classification/Measurement	CPU	DISK	TAPE	NETWORK	PRINT	Business Unit	etc
Online 1							
Online 2							
Time sharing 1							
Time sharing 2							
Batch 1							
Batch 2							
Total							

Figure C2: Measurement tools matrix

C.4 Define required system

Based on the Terms of Reference, the overall expectations of the cost management system should be outlined. The outline must include both business and management requirements.

C.5 Decide changes required

Compare the cost management capabilities currently available to the ones that are required to fulfil the requirements established above. Evaluate possible solutions that best accommodate the proposed changes.

Justify and document the feasible solutions; produce and submit a feasibility report to IT management for a decision.

C.6 Produce project plan

When agreement to go ahead is given produce a project plan for the rest of the project. The plan covers the:

* systems analysis and design phases (described in section 3.1 and in Annex D)

* development phase (described in section 4.1)

* implementation phase including testing (described in section 4.1)

* post-implementation phase (described in section 5.1).

It is advisable to specify in the project plans any uncertainties or risks which might jeopardise implementation. If necessary a formal risk analysis method (such as CCTA's CRAMM) can be employed.

Annex D. Major elements of a cost management system

This Annex provides a comprehensive description of a Computer Services Business Centre (CSBC) within which both revenues and expenditures are caused and controlled, such revenues and expenditures being used to evaluate CSBC performance. This system differs from that of a service cost centre (Utility Cost Centre - UCC) which exists only to provide a service or services to other cost centres. Whether it is decided to create a CSBC or UCC will depend upon the management requirements of your organization. Annex E provides further guidance on designing the CSBC.

Computer Service Business Centre/IT Utility Cost Centre

Whether setting up a CSBC or an IT UCC, there is a need to categorize costs for the purpose of calculating some form of unit cost or activity rate. There are five major different types of unit costs some direct, some indirect; shown in figure D1.

Figure D1: Unit cost types

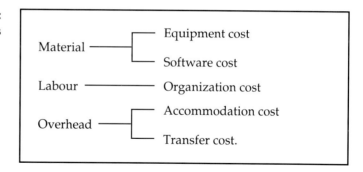

These unit costs denote an accumulation of element costs, as indicated in figure D2.

D.1 Outline system specification

Figure D2 provides a systems outline based on the Absorption Costing principle. If a marginal costing system was used, the amount of production overhead absorbed would relate to the variable element only.

D.2 Costing system overview

Figure D3 gives an overview of the main functions/activities of a CSBC.

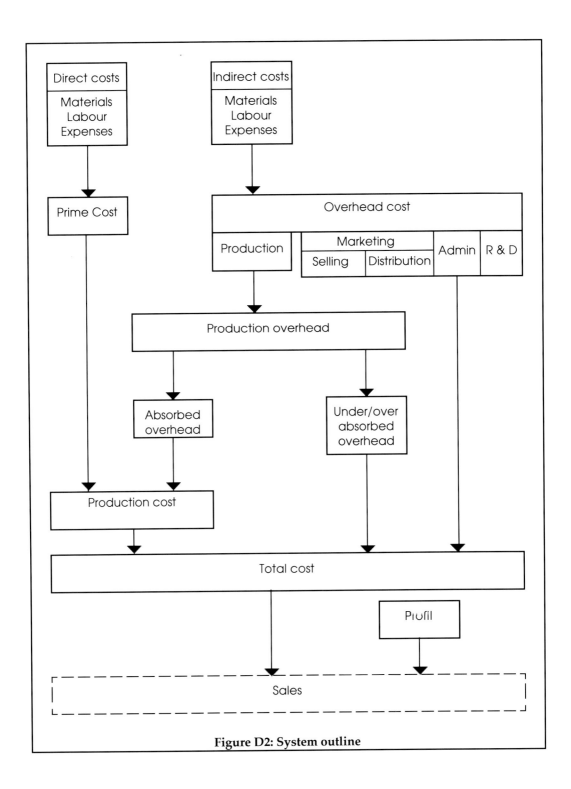

Figure D2: System outline

D.3 Decide cost unit

The first activity that must be performed by the CSBC is the classification of individual cost units. The purpose of this task is to order the cost elements so that rate calculations can be made.

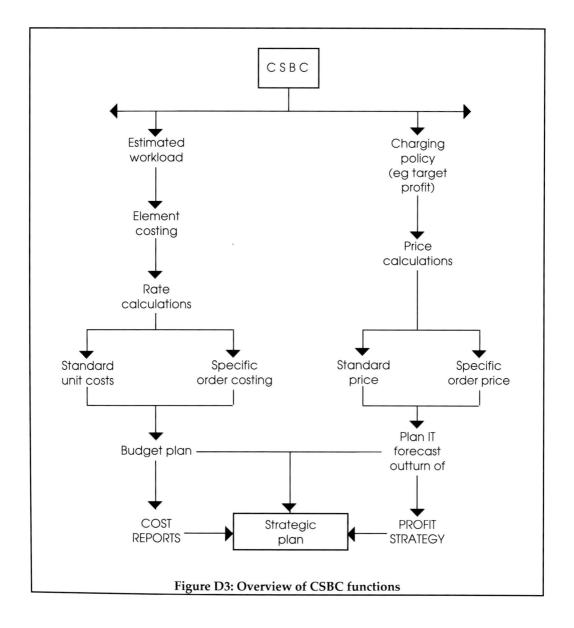

Figure D3: Overview of CSBC functions

IT cost units

The term IT cost units is used to denote an accumulation of costs for the purpose of calculating a unit cost or rate. There are five major different types of CSBC costs:

* equipment costs

* software costs

* organization costs

* accommodation costs

* transfer costs.

In practice not all the cost units mentioned above have to be used. Management must decide the appropriate functional headings under which to classify costs, depending upon the size and nature of the business. The amount of detailed costing information required will depend upon the aims and objectives of the costing and charging system introduced by the organization. Make sure that no matter how the functional cost units are set up, their total aggregation should equal the budgeted plan. A suggested content of costs covered by each functional unit is described below.

Equipment Cost Unit(ECU)

The ECU covers all IT hardware. Typical cost elements are:

* central processing

* disk storage devices

* tape devices

* communications networks (including terminals)

* printer systems.

Software Cost Unit (SCU)

System software costs cover all chargeable elements of costs both direct and indirect to operate the installation or to support the workloads as they run. Typical categories are:

* operating system components

* transaction processing systems

* database management systems

* operations scheduling systems

* capacity management systems

* accounting systems

* applications development software.

Organization Cost Unit (OCU)

Organizational costs are primarily staff costs and can be either direct or indirect, fixed or variable costs. This category also covers all expenditure associated with personnel, including training and travel. It can also include marketing costs, administration and research and development.

Accommodation Cost Unit (ACU)

Accommodation costs cover the expenditure for all environmental and accommodation requirements. Such costs can be direct or indirect. Typical elements are:

* machine room

* offices

* other facilities.

Transfer Cost Unit (TCU)

A transfer price is related to goods or other services transferred from one process or department to another, or from one member of a group to another. A transfer price may for example be based upon:

* marginal cost

* full cost

* market price

* negotiated price.

Cost Accounting (CA)

CA is used to establish budget and standard costs, actual costs of operations, processes, departments or products and analysis of variances and profitability.

D.4 Classification of costs

Costs must be classified into either Direct or Indirect costs, both for internal control purposes and production of the Profit and Loss Account. Direct costs for IT are those materials, labour and expense costs which can be applied directly to the IT service provided and which can be identified separately in the products' costs eg equipment, employee remuneration. Indirect costs are those costs which are not charged directly to a product or service eg buildings, insurance and water rates.

For estimating and control purposes costs can also be classified into either capital or current items of expenditure. Capital costs are typically associated with fixed assets such as land and buildings, plant and machinery (eg computer equipment).

Actual day-to-day costs of running the CSBC ie staff costs, hardware maintenance are current costs which relate to activities within a measured timeframe, usually annually.

The following list gives typical examples of the cost elements classified into capital spend and current expenditure (revenue spend) items:

Capital spend

* computer equipment

* building and plant

* software packages (not licensed).

Revenue spend

* staff costs

* maintenance of computer hardware and software

* suppliers and services rental fees for equipment

* software licence fees

* accommodation costs

* administration expenditures

* electricity, water, gas, rates

* disaster recovery

* consumables.

Depreciation

Depreciation is the measure of the wearing out, consumption or other reduction in the useful economic life of a fixed asset, whether from use, passage of time, or obsolescence through technological or market changes. Depreciation should be allocated so as to charge a fair proportion of cost or valuation of the asset to each accounting period expected to benefit from its use.

The assessment of depreciation, and its allocation to accounting periods, involves the consideration of three factors:

* the current cost (or valuation) of the asset

* the length of the asset's expected useful economic life to the business of the enterprise, having due regard to the incidence of obsolescence

* the estimated residual value of the asset at the end of its useful economic life in the business of the enterprise.

The useful economic life of an asset may be:

* pre-determined, as in the case of a lease

* dependent on its physical deterioration through use or passage of time

* reduced by economic or technological obsolescence.

Assessing depreciation

The depreciation methods used should be the ones most appropriate having regard to the types of assets and their use in the business.

The most common methods of assessing depreciation are:

* **straight line method** - where an equal amount is written-off the asset's value each year. Usually a fixed percentage of cost

* **reducing balance method** - where a set percentage is written-off the net book value each year. The net book value is the cost less depreciation written-off to date

* **by usage** - where depreciation is written-off according to the extent of usage during a period.

D.5 Workload estimating and forecasting

Workload estimating and forecasting is a prerequisite of budgeting. Estimates of workload volumes are normally obtained from historical data, and forecasts are made on the basis of updated information and revised plans. Such estimates and forecasts are required for the preparation of service level agreements and capacity management.

Workload estimates are required for each Cost Unit. In total, the workload estimates when costed should equal the budget for the year; workloads should be sub-totalled into three categories:

* direct work (prime costs)

* indirect work (overheads)

* transfer work (agreed cost).

There may also be workload estimates for indirect activities created by specific ad hoc tasks:

* direct work - is the workload specifically associated with end users

* indirect work - is the overheads that supports all the work performed on the system

* transfer work - is a good or service transferred from one process or department to another. To the extent that costs and profit are covered by the price is a matter of policy.

D.6 Standard Cost Calculation (SCC)

The SCCs are based upon the cost unit classification structure described in D4. The process of ascertaining the cost of an activity requires that for each element a cost is determined. Figure D4 describes the general flow and sequence of the individual rate calculations leading to the total standard cost for each unit function/activity.

A cost element rate is calculated by dividing the budgeted or estimated overhead cost attributable to a cost unit by either the number of cost outputs expected to be produced in the cost unit or by the number related to working at normal capacity.

For costing purposes, each cost element must be classified as either directly, or indirectly, attributable to the functional/activity unit specified by the CSBC Manager (eg the Equipment Cost Unit).

Prime Cost Factors are the total costs of the directly attributable materials, labour and expenses. The term prime cost is generally restricted only to direct production cost and does not customarily include direct costs pertaining to marketing or research and development.

Figure D4 describes the functions of the CSBC, and shows how the budgeted workload estimates are translated to standard cost rates per factor and element of activity. Definitions for each costing level are given below.

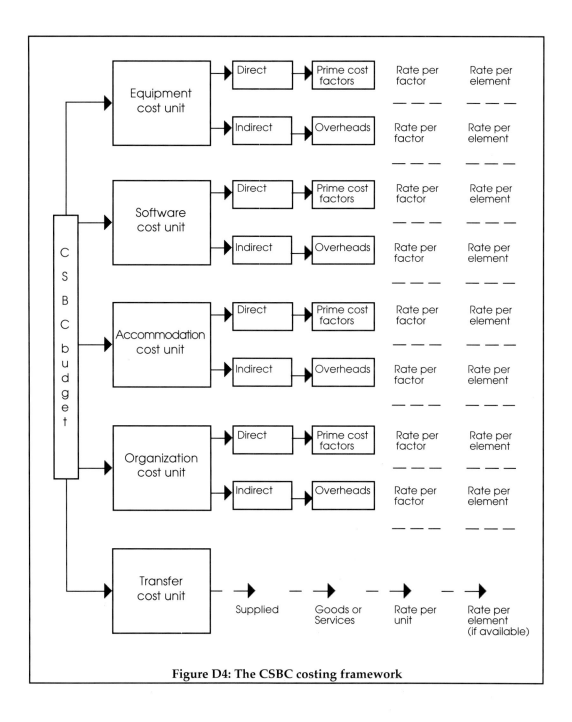

Figure D4: The CSBC costing framework

D.7 Standard cost units

The budgeting process invariably involves development of a standard costing system whereby resources are costed and apportioned or directly allocated on the basis of need; defined for these purposes as the achievement of predetermined objectives and plans. Standard costs, therefore, are derived to aid control of the organization by measuring actual performance against plans - as well as for charging purposes. Thus standard costs are an integral part of the budgeting process.

Figure D5 outlines a simple matrix in which the standard rate calculations by workload and equipment element (ie CPU, disks, tapes and networks) are recorded. This approach can be expanded for any number of services/elements.

Figure D5:
Standard unit costing

	CPU	DISK	TAPE	NETWORK
TSO				
CICS				
BATCH				
...				
...				

These standard costs are used in developing the CSBC Budget estimates/plan. As the financial year proceeds these standard costs are monitored and updated forecasts are made. By comparing standard costs to actual costs the CSBC Manager is better placed to focus action to either reduce costs or increase prices.

D.8 Select measurement units

Select the measurement units to be used in the cost management system. The measurements must provide data on the following:

* resource costs

* business components.

It is necessary to classify items such as hardware, tapes, business units and so on within the categories mentioned, so that appropriate yardsticks can be identified.

If, as is recommended, configuration management is functioning in the organization, the configuration management database (CMDB) will contain most of the required information.

Equipment measurement units

Before the introduction of multi-programming (the ability to run several computer programs concurrently) the simple measurement of elapsed time was used to determine system usage. The software supplied by manufacturers to identify system usage now reflects the use of multi-programming and can measure different forms of usage, which fundamentally can be classified as processor use and storage media use.

IBM software for example, utilizes the Systems Management Facility (SMF) and this software measures:

* CPU (Central Processing Unit) seconds

* number of Input/Output (I/O) actions by peripheral device

* main storage occupancy.

Similarly ICL software measures:

* OCP (Order Code Processor) seconds

* transfer to and from I/O devices.

Essentially, processors (OCP, CPU, disk drives, tape drives, printers and so on) actively perform work. Storage media (main store, disk store, tapes and paper) simply hold information. And because installations use both processors and storage devices it is important to be able to cost them independently so that plans to upgrade the devices can be accurately costed.

There are numerous unit measurements available for the work performed (CPU = seconds, print = lines, tape = I/Os and so on): it is therefore often difficult to apportion costs properly. How many CPU seconds equate to one tape I/O for example?

In many installations a mechanism is employed to reduce all measures of usage to two individual units, one for processors and one for storage.

The unit used for processors is often called **software work** and covers usage by processor type. The unit is merely a basic measure to which the variety of more commonly used measures can easily be converted.

The unit used for storage is often called **storage occupancy** covering usage by storage type.

Costs are allotted either to the software work or storage occupancy categories. The number of units of software work used for a program does not change with the multi-programming environment.

D.9   Worksheets

Figure D6 is an example of a cost centre worksheet which can be used to document the cost elements for rate calculations. The rate calculations also involve workload forecasts; Figure D7 is an example of a document used for workload forecast data.

Cost Centre name		Data centre:							Year:	
Account	Description of cost	Apr	May	Jun	Jul	...	Feb	Mar	Total	Monthly Avge.
Total per month										
Cost recovery per month										
Over (under) per month										
Cumulative total										
Cumulative cost recovery										
Cumulative over (under)										
Figure D6: Cost Centre worksheet										

Workload component		Data centre:					Metric:		Year:	
ECC No.	ECC name	Apr	May	Jun	Jul	...	Feb	Mar	Total	Monthly Avge.
	Totals									

Figure D7: Workload forecast data

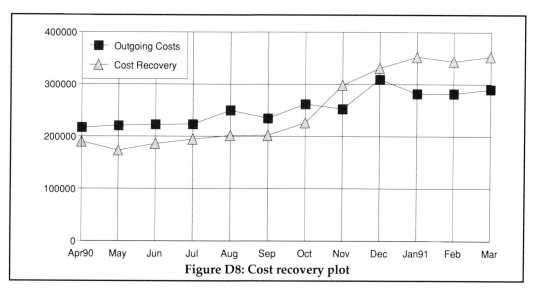

Figure D8: Cost recovery plot

Figures D8 and D9 represent cost recovery plots in graphical and tabular format. Given that individual ECU applied rates have been determined, these rates can be applied to the ECU workload forecasts to create projected monthly cost recovery plans. The cost recovery plans provide a valuable aid for obtaining a picture of break even points or periods of under (or over) recovery: it is also possible to observe and compare actual and planned costs. The comparison is invaluable if early corrective action is to be applied where recovered costs are at variance with the plan.

WORKLOADS					TOTALS			CUMULATIVE		
	BATCH	IMS	TSO	MENTEXT	Xfer	Recover	Cost	Varianc	Recover	Cost	Varianc
Apr-90	96231	30078	46781	12094	4598	189782	217201	-27419	189782	217201	-27419
May	87534	27327	42581	11004	4598	173044	220679	-47635	362826	437880	-75054
Jun	94495	29538	45977	11895	4598	186503	222541	-36038	549329	660421	-111092
Jul	98798	30871	48063	12449	4598	194779	223441	-28662	744108	883862	-139754
Aug	102367	31985	49767	12901	4598	201618	249939	-48321	945726	1133801	-188075
Sep	102453	32015	49822	12908	4987	202185	234709	-32524	1147911	1368510	-220599
Oct	115182	36001	56026	14498	4987	226694	262021	-35327	1374605	1630531	-255926
Nov	152454	47641	74195	19186	4987	298463	252678	45785	1673068	1883209	-210141
Dec	169549	52972	82453	21333	4987	331294	309709	21585	2004362	2192918	-188556
Jan-91	180685	56427	87853	22724	4987	352676	282541	70135	2357038	2475459	-118421
Feb	176066	55025	85615	22143	4987	343836	282539	61297	2700874	2757998	-57124
Mar	180817	56479	87935	22744	4987	352962	290321	62641	3053836	3048319	5517
TOTAL	1556631	486359	757068	195879	57899	3053836	3048319	5517	3053836	3048319	5517

Variance 0.18%

Figure D9: Cost recovery table

D.10 Alternate approaches to costing and charging

The guidance in Annex D (and in Annex E) has been distilled from cost management projects completed both in this country and the USA. The general guidelines and principles have been proven in use. However the actual systems analysis and design of the components of a cost management system which will satisfy the requirements of your organization may well differ. Provided your system is designed in accordance with sound principles of accountancy (and preferably with the advice of an accountant) it is not necessary to adhere to this particular design of a cost management system.

One method of charging (which is in use but is not recommended) involves establishing only the average cost of machine time and using this average as the charge for the resource.

Average cost

During any given period the total costs incurred are divided by the total number of hours used and the resultant cost per hour is charged to the user.

The main advantage of the method is that all computer department costs are recovered and a simple rate per hour of machine time is provided, which is apportioned equally across each user cost centre/branch. The main disadvantages to a user, however, are:

* only machine time is accounted for

* the rate for machine time can vary from period to period

* it is impossible to calculate job profitability on a regular basis

* costs to the user can fluctuate widely.

There are variances on this approach, again each of them limited to establishing a cost for machine time. They are included here for completeness.

Budgeted standard rate

Budgeted standard rate is based on an annual forecast of both operations department costs and machine load. The resultant rate is then fixed for a period of a year.

The formula is:

Budget Total Costs
Budget Total Hours

The advantages of the system are:

* that a consistent rate is used for a whole year

* job costing is easier

* **period** by **period** comparisons can be made.

The disadvantages, however, are that machine loading has a direct bearing on the cost of a job: the same job on the same machine, but with a different load would cost a completely different amount.

The current installation life of the equipment has a direct bearing on the rate. Thus, recently installed equipment tends to be lightly loaded giving a high average cost, while a machine just about to be upgraded and, therefore, heavily loaded, gives rise to a low average rate. The major flaw in this method, therefore, is that as usage increases so the cost of machine time per hour decreases. The effect is to show reducing costs when, in fact, no such decrease is actually taking place.

*Budgeted standard rate
using a standard machine*

The use of budgeted standard rate on a standard machine is a refinement of the standard rate described above and is an attempt to overcome the disadvantages which are produced by that method. The rate is not based on the actual forecast machine usage but rather on use of a machine at an average load. For the purposes of calculation this is defined as shifts (time bands), and all related costs (eg staff and all variable costs) are calculated on the same level of activity. The effect is to fix the costs of machine time at what should reflect a "market rate".

The method is often refined further by calculating the costs based on a balanced machine. Thus, when installed, central processors may be under-utilized due to the number of peripherals. Estimates can be made of a probable optimum configuration and the resultant additional costs **and** throughput potential added to the calculation.

The advantage of using the method described is that a constant machine rate is obtained, which is not influenced by the actual equipment installed. The advantages described for the previous method (the standard rate method) are also applicable.

Annex E. Design

E.1 Outline design process

This annex provides an overview of the components that normally make up the costing and charging parts of the cost management system. Figure E1 outlines the design process needed to produce the blueprints for the system to be implemented. The annex describes some of the possible outputs from a cost management system, and some of the possible design considerations.

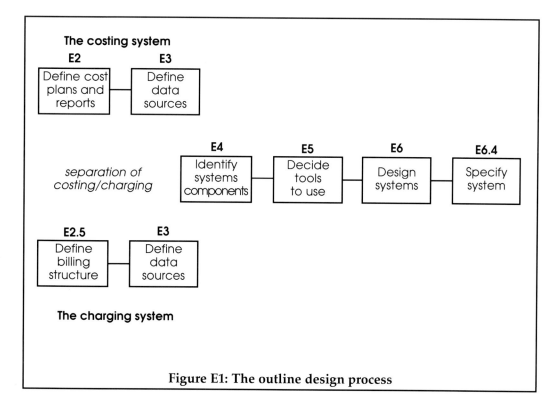

Figure E1: The outline design process

E.2 Define cost plans and reports

This section comprises examples of management plans, reports and procedures needed to ensure that the costing and charging objectives of a cost management function are fulfilled as a natural part of the IT infrastructure management. A few practical examples, by way of illustration are given where they are useful.

The Profit and Loss account

Two of the major documents are the Tactical Plan (Budget) and the profit and Loss Account.

The aim of the Profit and Loss Account (or Operating Account) is to match the cost (or value) of resources consumed in a financial period with the income earned in that period, with a view to identifying a surplus or loss for that period.

It is necessary for the CSBC profit and loss account to show the total revenue generated and the expenditure incurred in providing the IT services.

It is important that the Tactical Plan/Budgets and the profit and loss account, when produced, are capable of reconciliation.

An example of a Profit and Loss Account is given in figure E2.

COMPUTER SERVICES BUSINESS CENTRE
PROFIT AND LOSS ACCOUNT FOR THE YEAR ENDED ___/___/___

	Expenditure	Income
Turnover*		X
Cost of Services sold*		(X)
GROSS PROFIT		X
Selling and Distribution costs*	X	
Administration expenses*	X	
		(X)
Other Income receivable*		X
PROFIT ON ORDINARY ACTIVITIES BEFORE TAXATION		X
Tax on profit on ordinary activities		(X)
PROFIT FOR THE FINANCIAL YEAR		X
Profit and Loss Account balance b/fwd		X
PROFIT AND LOSS ACCOUNT BALANCE C/FWD		X

Note
* Detailed as appropriate

Figure E2: Example Profit & Loss Account

The balance sheet

A balance sheet is a statement of the financial position of an entity at a given date disclosing the value of the assets, utilities and so on. The balance sheet is prepared to give a true and fair view of the state of the entity at that date. An example is shown in figure E3.

COMPUTER SERVICES BUSINESS CENTRE
BALANCE SHEET AS AT ___/___/___

	£	£	Totals £

FIXED ASSETS
Intangible Assets
a)   Development costs   X
b)   Concessions, Patents, Licences,   X
       Trade Marks etc   X
Tangible Assets
a)   Land and Buildings   X
b)   Plant and Machinery   X
c)   Fixtures, fittings, tools and equipment   X
                                                                                                            X
Investments   X
                                                                                                            X

CURRENT ASSETS
a)   Stocks   X
b)   Debtors   X
c)   Cash at bank and in hand   X
                                                                                                            X

CREDITORS: AMOUNTS FALLING DUE WITHIN ONE YEAR
a)   Bank loans and overdrafts   X
b)   Trade creditors   X
c)   Payment received on account   X
d)   Other creditors including taxation and social security   X
                                                                                                    (X)
NET CURRENT ASSETS   X
TOTAL ASSETS LESS CURRENT LIABILITIES   X

FINANCED BY.
CREDITORS: AMOUNTS FALLING DUE AFTER MORE THAN ONE YEAR
a)   Bank loans and overdrafts   X
b)   Trade creditors   X
c)   Payments received on account   X
d)   Other creditors including taxation and social security   X
                                                                                                            X

PROVISION FOR LIABILITIES AND CHARGES
a)   Deferred taxation   X
b)   Pensions   X
                                                                                                            X
ACCRUALS AND DEFERRED INCOME   X
CAPITAL AND RESERVES
a)   Reserves   X
b)   Profit and loss account balance   X   X
                                                                                                            X

Figure E3: Example Balance sheet

IT Tactical Plan *(Cost Section)*								
Item	Apr-90	May-90	Jun-90	Jul-90	...	Feb-91	Mar-91	Total
Income								
Business support	265.9	274.8	283.9	293.4	...	369.1	381.4	3845.9
Admin Support	193.8	198.3	202.9	207.7	...	244.1	249.8	2648.5
IT Development	159.5	161.5	163.5	165.6	...	180.6	182.9	2051.2
Total Income	**619.2**	**634.6**	**650.4**	**666.6**	**...**	**793.8**	**814.0**	**8545.7**
Expenditures								
Hardware								
depreciation			680.1		...		680.1	2720.4
hire	26.7	27.0	27.4	27.7	...	30.2	30.6	343.4
maintenance	26.2	26.4	26.6	26.9	...	28.5	28.7	329.2
Software								
rental	30.9	30.9	30.9	30.9	...	30.9	30.9	370.8
Accommodation								
buildings			67.8		...		67.8	271.2
maintenance	18.7	18.9	19.0	19.2	...	20.3	20.5	235.0
consumables	12.6	12.7	12.8	12.9	...	13.7	13.8	158.3
power etc.			72.8		...		75.6	296.9
Organization								
salaries	284.5	286.6	288.8	290.9	...	306.6	308.9	3558.4
administration	9.2	9.3	9.4	9.4	...	10.0	10.1	115.6
training	12.2	12.2	12.2	12.2	...	12.2	12.2	146.4
Total Expenditure	**421.0**	**424.0**	**1247.8**	**430.1**	**...**	**452.4**	**1279.2**	**8545.6**
Profit (loss)	**198.2**	**210.6**	**(597.4)**	**236.5**	**...**	**341.4**	**(465.1)**	**0.1**
Cumulative	**198.2**	**408.8**	**(188.6)**	**47.9**	**...**	**465.2**	**0.1**	

Figure E4: Example Tactical plan extract

IT tactical plan

The IT tactical plan is the planning counterpart to the profit and loss statement. The income and expenditure elements should be structured in the same way so that actuals can easily be compared with plans. Figure E4 provides an example extract of the cost section from an IT Tactical Plan.

Cost forecast in IT Strategic Plan *(costs to be recovered)*								
	1989/90		1990/91		1991/92		1992/93	1993/94
	Per unit	£ Total	Per unit	£ Total	Per unit	£ Total	£ Total	£ Total
Business support								
Licences	0.081	576,535	0.077	634,772	0.077	767,920	879,613	1,084,642
General DB	0.781	435,725	0.742	479,739	0.739	580,367	664,781	819,735
Distribution	0.668	1,827,350	0.635	2,011,936	0.628	2,433,951	2,787,968	3,437,816
Search	1.390	499,525	1.321	549,983	1.314	665,346	762,120	939,763
Marketing	0.559	258,910	0.531	285,063	0.529	344,857	395,016	487,091
Stock control	0.187	429,835	0.178	473,254	0.176	572.522	655.795	808.654
Admin. support								
Personnel	15.9	126,755	15.105	139,581	14.981	168,859	193,419	238,503
Building	n/a	36,894	n/a	40,621	n/a	49,141	56,289	69,409
Finance	502.0	105,256	476.9	115,888	473.662	140,196	160,588	198,019
Client services	0.658	73,685	0.625	81,128	0.620	98,145	112,420	138,625
IT support								
Development	24,164	627,866	22,955.8	691,288	22,722.9	836,290	957,928	1,181,212
Install'n Mgmt	15,865	128,761	15,071.8	141,768	14,976.7	171,504	196,449	242,240
DC support	506.62	86,265	481.29	94,979	476.76	114,901	131,614	162,291
Totals		5,213,382		5,740,000		6,944,000	7,954,000	9,808,000
Figure E5: Element cost projection								

Government Departments and Non-Departmental Public Bodies should also refer to the HM Treasury publication "Trading Accounts: A Guide for Government Departments and Non-Departmental Public Bodies", for additional advice on the preparation of accounts. The private sector should produce accounts that conform to the format set out in The Companies Acts 1985 and 1989.

Cost forecasts in the IT strategic plan

The planning and related costing information can be grouped in three ways:

* an element cost projection relating to the rate structure (figure E5)

* a cost unit expenditure projection (figure E6)

* capital expenditure projection (figure E7).

In each case, the planning information is used as estimated costs against which actuals are measured to test the effectiveness of the costing system.

Cost Forecast in IT Strategic Plan *(Cost Centre Forecast)*					
Cost Centre Forecast	1989/90	1990/91	1991/92	1992/93	1993/94
Equipment costs					
CPU	925,334	1,062,000			
DISK	425,096	508,000			
TAPE	46,612	94,000			
COMMS	805,108	1,010,000			
PRINTER	226,352	142,000			
Total	2,428,502	2,816,000	3,368,000	4,120,000	5,368,000
Software costs	331,894	524,000	910,000	920,000	990,000
Accommodation costs	721,986	296,000	290,000	312,000	350,000
Organization costs	1,731,000	2,104,000	2,376,000	2,602,000	3,100,000
Totals	5,213,382	5,740,000	6,944,000	7,954,000	9,808,000
Increase on previous year		10.1%	20.98%	14.54%	23.31%
The percentage which these costs represent of the total IT costs	64%	66%	69%	70%	72%

Figure E6: Cost unit expenditure projection

Define invoicing structure

Annex D (D.9 and D.11) discussed the pricing policies to be considered before the invoicing structure is defined. The invoicing structure is in most cases a combination of the elements of fixed service prices and unit prices (business and resource).

As an example, consider an organization in which the IT costing has established total costs of £1.7 million and it has been decided to make a profit of £0.3m. The total cost to be recovered is therefore £2m.

A policy decision is first of all taken that half of that figure is recovered through fixed priced services. The fixed price is then calculated from the number of services offered and the number of users connecting to each. An example of a fixed price service outside IT is British Rail season tickets: a payment is made for the season ticket and, so far as the purchase price is concerned, it is irrelevant to BR how many times it is used.

Capital Expenditure Plan					
Capital expenditure	1989/90	1990/91	1991/92	1992/93	1993/94
CPUs					
Upgrade	212,000	648,000	572,000	750,000	540,000
New mainframe		3,000,000	7,500,000		12,450,000
Disks					
Centre 1	286,000	146,000			675,000
Centre 2		583,000	875,000	125,000	940,000
Tape					
Centre 2		114,000	212,000		175,000
Communications					
Controllers	112,000	158,000	150,000	150,000	150,000
VDUs	85,000	100,000	100,000	100,000	100,000
Network printers	45,000	45,000	75,000	75,000	75,000
Miscellaneous					
	100,000	100,000	100,000	100,000	100,000
TOTALS	840,000	4,894,000	9,584,000	1,300,000	15,205,000
Figure E7: Capital expenditure projection					

An IT example could be the allocation of dedicated testing slots, used by systems programmers, for which there is a fixed fee.

The organization must now recover a further £1m through business unit and resource unit charging. If the organization is serving development and business users equally, it may decide to split the remaining cost recovery between the two raising £0.5m from each group.

Based on historical information, the forecast number of on-line work sessions and resources consumed is used to fix the resource unit pricing structure so that £0.5m is recovered.

Similarly, business forecasts are used to determine the business unit prices and thus fund the raising of the remaining costs.

A unit price example outside IT is again found in BR where individual tickets are sold for a specific journey. A resource unit example is a seat reservation.

Section 5 of this module covers adjustment that may be necessary to the set charges, but it is worth reiterating that alterations in:

*   service levels

*   business forecasts

*   manpower

*   capacity

*   demand

all may affect the actual costs and therefore the charging algorithms. Whether or not the organization wishes to alter the charges if costs are affected is another issue discussed in section 5.

E.3 Define data sources

Data recording

Identify the data elements and the sources to be used to provide information on workloads, resource usage and costs. Document the data layout for each type of rate measurement to be used and identify and establish the procedures required to obtain the information on a regular basis.

Define inventory schedule

Consolidate and structure the cost information. Except for organization cost centres (personnel), this cost information should be available in fixed asset registers, from configuration management or from similar sources of organizational accounting information. The primary function of the Inventory Schedule (IS) is to prepare the information and present it in a uniform format to make the rate calculations straightforward. Additionally, the IS provides a valuable means of verifying actual expenditures and of checking the status (eg whether or not ordered equipment has been installed, whether or not an item requires maintenance) of the various resources. Identify and establish the procedures required to gather the information on a regular basis.

Determine planning input

Select from the various sources of next year's workload plans the data and format to be used. Estimates are the basis of your planning data for the coming financial year. The information should be available from service level management or capacity management. Where possible, identify a workload specific to a user: where this cannot be done, ensure that the usage of the workload is clearly identified. Identify and establish the procedures required to get workload information on a regular basis.

E.4 Identify systems components

Produce a system diagram covering the systems components needed to fulfil the requirements specifications established as part of the systems analysis. Figures E8 and E9 give an overview of the components usually necessary. It is important that the design recognizes that processes in the cost management system are carried out at regular intervals appropriate to the organization.

The costing part of the system is concerned with:

* annual planning of estimated costs

* predicting the size of the workloads

* the quality of the services that justify the costs

* the recording and management of the actual costs as they occur.

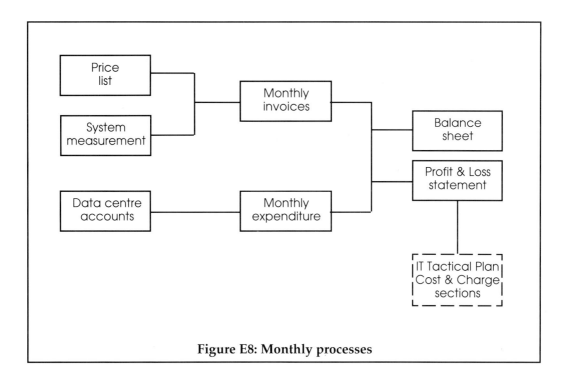

Figure E8: Monthly processes

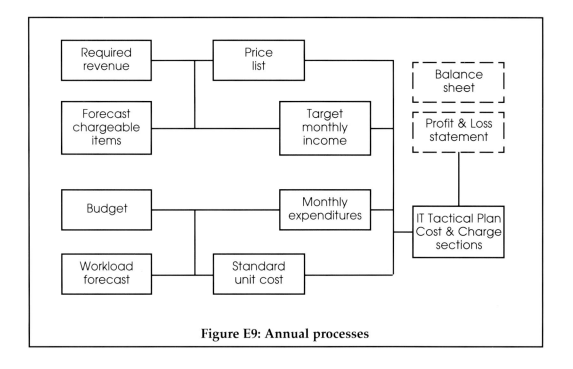

Figure E9: Annual processes

The charging part is concerned with:

*   the setting of prices

*   the raising of charges as services are provided

*   the collection of money, all based on an established charging policy.

E.5 Decide tools to be used

It is necessary to decide on the tools and other supporting facilities, eg languages to be used for the systems.

A combination of integrated measurement tools and databases in the mainframe environment, and PC spreadsheets and graphics, all linked together by a common data flow is likely to be needed.

E.6 Design systems

Identify IT cost centres

Select the IT cost unit structure most suitable for your organization. Although the choice of most cost units is obvious, eg hardware and software, great care must be taken to keep the structure simple but meaningful. In managing the cost units ensure that they are meaningful in business terms.

Customize worksheets

Decide the level of details to be used in the plans and reports and ensure that the same structures are used for the worksheets and for the computer inputs. Common structuring enables data to be transferred from paper to electronic media more easily. It is very important to decide on these structures and to get agreement from all the parties involved, as it is extremely difficult to change the design later.

Tailor the example work sheets (figures D6 and D7 found in Annex D) which are required to process the cost and workload data, by establishing relevant workload and equipment elements. Remember that this is equipment **elements** (not the Equipment Cost Unit); the purpose of establishing classifications is to define a **single** structure (the matrix shown in Annex D.7) which is then used for the entry of information being developed in the rate calculations (Annex D.6), using the major classifications (ECC, SCC, OCC, ACC and TCC, Annex D.3).

Design individual components

Design the functions, inputs and outputs of each of the system components identified in E.4 and throughout Annex D.

Annex D provides all of the guidance necessary for a decision to be made about the type of costing system to be designed, and the options available for deciding cost centres.

The charging system is trialled against actual data to gain information about how well the charges will meet the organization's objectives, and to gain experience of the relationship between costs and charges and how they affect customer behaviour.

System specifications

The functional systems specification should be drawn up using SSADM guidelines so that deliverables can be clearly identified and approved at the appropriate management level. Deliverables include examples of worksheets, invoices, price lists, cost plans and all of the other functions discussed throughout Annexes D and E, which it has been decided to adopt for the system to be implemented in your organization.

Implementation

Decide upon the best method of implementing the chosen system, taking account of the guidance outlined in section 4 of this module. It is important to consider the security of the costing/charging system (as is the case with **all** IT systems) and to ensure that access restrictions, for example, are defined. An appropriate time-window for implementation must be identified; it is useful to align implementation to the start of the financial year. A fall-back position should be established, with accounts to be maintained manually should problems arise with the new system (see below).

*Testing and
parallel running*

In section 3.1 of this module, it is recommended that the new system is piloted through its first year of operation, both to gain confidence in the system and to allow for the possibility of errors being discovered. Nevertheless, even this prudence may not be sufficient to eradicate all problems and it is recommended that a manual system is specified, which runs in parallel to the pilot cost management system for a period of time (about three months) to ensure that the manual system is practical and accurate. It is recommended that the operational plan for cost management examines a fall-back option in case the software tools (or PC!) are lost. Clearly, if the organization must have the information, it must also have a contingency plan insuring against loss of the information.

CCTA hopes that you find this book both useful and interesting. We will welcome your comments and suggestions for improving it.
Please use this form or a photocopy, and continue on a further sheet if needed.

From:

Name

Organization

Address

Telephone

COVERAGE
Does the material cover your needs?
If not, then what additional material would you like included.

CLARITY
Are there any points which are unclear?
If yes, please detail where and why.

ACCURACY
Please give details of any inaccuracies found.

If more space is required for these or other comments, please continue overleaf.

OTHER COMMENTS

Return to: **Information Systems Engineering Group**
CCTA,
Rosebery Court,
St Andrews Business Park,
Norwich, NR7 0HS

Further information

Further information on the contents of this module can be obtained from:

Information Systems Engineering Group
CCTA
Rosebery Court
St Andrews Business Park
Norwich
NR7 0HS

Telephone: 01603 704704
(GTN: 3040 4704)

The price of this publication has been set to make a contribution to the costs incurred by CCTA in preparing the copy.

Printed in the United Kingdom for The Stationery Office
TJ731 C7 3/00 10170